PRACTICAL SOCIAL WORK

Series Editor: Jo Campling

BASW

Social work is at an important stage in its development. All professions must be responsive to changing social and economic conditions if they are to meet the needs of those they serve. This series focuses on sound practice and the specific contribution which social workers can make to the well-being of our society.

The British Association of Social Workers has always been conscious of its role in setting guidelines for practice and in seeking to raise professional standards. The conception of the Practical Social Work series arose from a survey of BASW members to discover where they, the practitioners in social work, felt there was the most need for new literature. The response was overwhelming and enthusiastic, and the result is a carefully planned, coherent series of books. The emphasis is firmly on practice set in a theoretical framework. The books will inform, stimulate and promote discussion, thus adding to the further development of skills and high professional standards. All the authors are practitioners and teachers of social work representing a wide variety of experience.

JO CAMPLING

A list of published titles in this series follows overleaf

PRACTICAL SOCIAL WORK

Women, Management and Care

Cordelia Grimwood

and

Ruth Popplestone

with a chapter by Julia Phillipson

MACMILLAN

First published 1993 by
THE MACMILLAN PRESS LTD
Houndmills, Basingstoke, Hampshire RG21 2XS
and London
Companies and representatives
throughout the world

ISBN 0-333-55147-8 hardcover
ISBN 0-333-55148-6 paperback

A catalogue record for this book
is available from the British Library.

Copy-edited and typeset by Povey–Edmondson
Okehampton and Rochdale, England

Printed in Hong Kong

Series Standing Order (Practical Social Work)

If you would like to receive future titles in this series as they are published, you can make use of our standing order facility. To place a standing order please contact your bookseller or, in case of difficulty, write to us at the address below with your name and address and the name of the series. Please state with which title you wish to begin your standing order. (If you live outside the UK we may not have the rights for your area, in which case we will forward your order to the publisher concerned.)

Standing Order Service, Macmillan Distribution Ltd,
Houndmills, Basingstoke, Hampshire, RG21 2XS, England

Contents

v

Acknowledgements

We owe a profound debt to all the women with whom we have worked and those we have met on courses and at conferences. Without their support and inspiration, this book could not have been written.

We thank WISE (Women in Social Work Education) who devoted part of a meeting to discussing the subject matter of this book at a critical time.

Thank you to Barbara Warner, Isabella Angers and the late John Gee for support and companionship. Thank you to Joan Fletcher, Julia Phillipson and Nomi Rowe for their helpful comments on the draft. Thank you to Judy Foster for being the best possible job sharer of a management post. Thank you to Ann Davis for supervising some of the research.

We are grateful to the following men for their example in opposing sexism in various contexts: Harry Marsh, now director of 'Contact-a-Family'; Gerry Popplestone, writer; and John Grigg, Leader of Hounslow Council 1986–7.

Finally, we gratefully acknowledge help with computing from Derek Cohen, freelance computer expert, and Rae Beaver and Alan Hooker at the Computer Centre of the University of East London; also Anna Bass and her team at the Reprographic Centre UEL for photocopying.

London   CORDELIA GRIMWOOD
                                              RUTH POPPLESTONE

1

Setting the Scene

Some years ago an American school teacher undertook an interesting experiment. Her pupils learned something about the effects of prejudice which they would remember for the rest of their lives.

She divided her class according to whether the children had blue or brown eyes. She proceeded to treat each group very differently. She behaved towards one of the groups as though they were superior, giving them a lot of praise, encouragement and rewards, and told them how good they were. She treated the other group as though they were unintelligent, less valuable, unimportant, useless, and deprived them of the things they enjoyed, such as play time. Not surprisingly, the effect was that the children responded to her behaviour as though they were indeed different, like a self-fulfilling prophesy. The teacher also did similar work with adults, with the same results. It was a powerful experience for everyone.

If this teacher had been called in to work with a personal social services organisation, she might have devised a training exercise in which all the people in the group with red hair played the role of manager for a day and she would have repeatedly conveyed to them how important they were, how intelligent, how powerful, and hence deserving greater rewards than anyone else (ABC News, 1970). If such an idea were translated into real life, it would be regarded as ridiculous: there are relatively few people with red hair, and they have no particular claim to management skills.

Yet we do have such a situation in the personal social services. The majority of the staff in these organisations are

1

women, but most of the managers are men. For example, seven out of eight staff in Social Services Departments in England and Wales are women, but seven out of eight directors are men (SSI, 1991). What causes such an extraordinary state of affairs?

We will start off by looking at staffing figures in a little more detail. Unfortunately, very little information is available now. Before 1977 the Department of Health and Social Security (DHSS) used to publish information on the numbers of men and women in management posts at different levels. At that time the numbers of men and women in first line management posts in Social Services Departments was about equal (DHSS, 1976). Above that, the proportion of women to men in more senior management positions fell off rapidly. Figures for this group of staff are still collected by Manpower Watch (SSI, 1991), and they show that the gender breakdown has remained more or less the same.

The lowest paid workers in clerical and care posts are overwhelmingly female, and a high proportion of them work part time (SSI, 1991). From our observation, most of the black and ethnic minority workers employed are in these lower grades. There are hardly any black people at senior levels, and those in professional jobs are frequently in specialist posts, often recruited to work with black consumers.

Forty-four of the 116 Social Services Departments in England and Wales have no women at all in senior management (SSI, 1991). There are only thirty-three with more than one woman senior manager (SSI, 1991). From observation, we have noted that most of the top jobs in voluntary organisations are being taken over by men, probably because much higher salaries are now being offered.

Councillors in local authorities and committee members in voluntary organisations are responsible for formulating the policies of these organisations, which affect their staff and the consumers of their services. A survey of all local authorities in Britain carried out in 1985 (West Midlands County Council Women's subcommittee) showed that only 19.4 per cent of councillors were women and only 0.4 per cent of these were black. Very few of them were chairing committees. Other surveys show that only 3.5 per cent of councils in England and

Wales had a woman leader of the council (300 Group, 1989). Women are seriously under-represented as chairs of committees (Angela Coyle, 1989). We are thus faced with a situation where decisions about policy in the personal social services are being made almost entirely by white men. They control a workforce in which the vast majority of the rest of the staff are women, particularly those who work directly with consumers of the service. The consumers themselves are more often women, reflecting the fact that two-thirds of very elderly people are women, as are 90 per cent of single parents. Also women are generally expected to take responsibility for family problems and are more likely to be available during the day to see social workers. In some groups of consumers black people are over-represented, for example, children in care and in day nurseries, and young people on probation. Most unpaid as well as paid carers are also women, as are most volunteers.

In summary, although caring and support roles in the personal social services are overwhelmingly in the hands of women, power and control of these organisations is retained by white men. The results of this state of affairs are that:

● Women's talents are being wasted
● Women are suffering discrimination
● Important decisions are being taken by men
● Organisations are being run to suit men.

We will examine each of these points briefly now, and we will be returning to them in later chapters.

Women's talents are being wasted

Few women are getting the chance to progress beyond first line management. This means that men in the personal social services stand an excellent chance of being promoted. It is obviously much easier for the few men to get promotion than if they were working in organisations which employed mostly men. This must affect the quality of managers, because such a small proportion of the workforce is being promoted. The small number of qualified men in Social Services Departments is diminishing (SSI, 1991). Between 1977 and 1988 the number of male fieldworkers fell from over a third of the total to a quarter. The number of men applying for places on social work training courses is decreasing. The implications of this will become more serious because the fall in the birthrate means that fewer people are now entering the labour market. If women continue not to be appointed to management posts, standards of management may decline even further, despite the fact that there is a vast reserve of untapped talent.

The 'Peter principle' has long been evident in the personal social services as well as other organisations (Laurence Peter, 1971). This means that people get promoted to a level at which they subsequently stay because they are working ineffectively and cannot get further promotion: effective work is done by those lower down in the organisation. While men tend to be promoted to levels beyond their competence, women are held in posts below their level of competence. This has become known as the 'Paula principle'. Most people in the personal social services are familiar with situations where women are working effectively but are being managed by men who are working ineffectively. This obviously affects the quality of the whole service. Sometimes ineffective managers are propped up by the staff they are supposed to be managing, very often by efficient secretaries.

Women are suffering discrimination

Despite the Sex Discrimination Act (1975) and equal opportunities policies, women are still not getting their fair share of high-status, well-paid jobs. Some people could object that this is because they do not apply. If this is true, it is necessary to look more closely at the reasons.

Important decisions are being taken by men

Policy for women consumers and women workers in the personal social services is being made by men. The people whom these services affect are largely not consulted and their needs are often misunderstood, as we shall see in later chapters. It is beginning to be recognised that in order to achieve an ethnically sensitive service, black and ethnic minority workers must be employed at all levels. It is still not recognised that for a service or an organisation to be sensitive to the needs of women, their views must be listened to and acted upon (Daphne Statham, 1990). This will only happen if they are in positions of authority.

Organisations are being run to suit men

Personal social services organisations have always been controlled by men, so it is not surprising that they are run in ways that suit men. Women have for many years felt isolated and out of place in situations where they are outnumbered by men. Sometimes they have mistakenly blamed themselves for these feelings. It is only recently that women have started exchanging notes and discussing these problems at training courses, conferences and with colleagues. They have discovered that their experiences of working with men are remarkably similar. The same issues are raised and similar examples reported by women from many different organisations all over the country. Increasingly, women are also writing about their experiences at work and people are carrying out research on matters connected with gender at work.

Where possible we have based this book on research findings. All the other statements we make are drawn both from our own experiences and from those of women we have met or worked with over many years, or read about in social work journals. It is very striking how similar are the comments through a range of workplaces. The statements are also consistent with the ever-growing research and anecdotal evidence from women's domestic and family lives. As Jalna Hanmer and Daphne Statham (1988) point out, there is a range of commonalities between women workers and women consumers on account of their position in society.

Increasingly, women are discovering that what they have been brought up to believe about themselves, and what they hear and see in the media about women, is not actually true in their own experience. In all areas women are redefining their lives and reconsidering how they want to lead them. This book is an attempt to present to both men and women a picture of how a sizeable number of women in the personal social services are seeing and experiencing their situation.

Because our language reflects the experience of men, it is not always easy to find the right words to describe women's experience. Men's ways of thinking and men's language are often inadequate as a means of expressing the way in which women view the world and feel about their situation. Women need to develop a language and philosophy of their own to make sense of it.

We are aware that there will be many people, women as well as men, who do not agree with our viewpoint. There will be those who think we exaggerate and overstate our case. There will also be some who think we are being too mild. We have tried to create a balance. We have also tried hard not to misrepresent the experience of black women, disabled women and lesbians, but we recognise that our understanding of their issues is inadequate. We also believe that each group must speak for itself, and we see this book as only part of that process.

We freely admit that our statements about women and men are generalisations, and that there are exceptions to these. We have already mentioned some of these in the Acknowledgements. What we are sure of is that many women and a few men will agree with most of what we have written. It is, after all, based on what very many women have said and written.

We are not suggesting that all women should aim to be managers: what we want is for all women to have more of a choice in the matter. We would like all women to take their paid work seriously and to consider and decide for themselves what balance they want between paid work and their personal lives. We would also like women to be taken seriously and respected in the workplace, and for those who wish to make their contribution in management, to be respected for it, and to be encouraged to achieve their full potential.

Central to personal social services organisations is the concept of caring. We begin the next chapter by examining what is meant by caring, and why caring work is strongly associated with women, to such an extent that it has become known as 'women's work'. People who decide to work in the personal social services often do not realise the amount of 'control' that is involved in social work and social care. The themes of care and control are central to this book, and in Chapter 3 we take a historical view of the development of women's work with reference to care and control.

Although the control element is played down by the public image of the personal social services, it is very prominent in the way management is practised, to the neglect of what is becoming popularly known as 'staff care' and 'customer care'. This leads to a culture clash in organisations, which we examine in Chapter 4.

Women's jobs and careers in the personal social services pattern themselves differently from those of men, and we look at these patterns in Chapter 5. The main route to management posts for both women and men is by means of career ladders. In Chapters 5 and 6 we examine some of the problems facing women who try to climb the ladders.

In Chapter 7 we look at what it is like to be a woman manager in personal social services organisations. Women managers face a number of common dilemmas that do not affect men. One of these is management style, which assumes a crucial importance for many women. Chapter 8 is devoted to this topic.

One of the aspects of management style which is most problematic to women is handling power. We continue this theme in Chapter 9, which examines how power is used and abused. Chapter 10 concludes the book with suggestions for strategies to encourage more women into management.

We have quoted other authors' names in full during the text, for two reasons. Firstly we want to recognise as fully as possible the contribution of other women to our subject. Secondly, we wish to challenge the male public school tradition of referring to people by their surnames only.

2

Women's Work, Care and Control

The focus of this book is on women managers in the personal social services. In order to understand the present situation, it is important to be aware of the historical and social contexts, because they explain what is happening now.

The situation in which women managers find themselves at the present time is the result of two main factors. The first of these is the whole notion of 'caring' and how this has become part of being a woman in our society and therefore been downgraded and devalued; also how women have been confined to caring roles. In this chapter we trace the development of women as carers and examine what is meant by caring. The emphasis on caring in the personal social services has exacerbated the split between the care and control aspects. So women coming into social work are often surprised by or uncomfortable with the control function of social work. On the other hand, men tend to be attracted to the control aspects of the work and by opportunities to gain quick promotion as managers. Thus the structure of the personal social services mirrors that of society as a whole, in that women are relegated to caring functions.

The second strand is historical. In Chapter 3 we describe how over the years men have 'managed' all employment organisations, being serviced by women at home, and more recently by women in support positions at work. We describe the development of the caring side of social work and also the control aspects, of which management is only one. The struggle women are engaged in to establish themselves in management at the present time reflects this background, which we trace in the next two chapters.

Caring

Anyone looking for a job in the personal social services will notice how often the words 'care' and 'caring' crop up in the advertisements. Captions such as 'Do you care?'; 'Doncaster cares'; 'Care at the heart of the patch' compete for attention from prospective applicants. Recent advertisements ask for 'qualified carers', 'head of care', 'a caring manner', 'caring people' in a wide range of posts. Phrases such as 'social care', 'child care', 'residential care', 'care in the community', are part of the everyday language of the personal social services. What exactly do we mean by caring? Why do women do the caring in our society? These are questions which we will examine in this chapter.

The identity of women in this culture, as in most others, is tied to caring. By caring we mean the physical and emotional support that women give others as part of their daily activities. The physical caring activities involve feeding, cleaning, shopping, organising, tidying, laundering and taking care of clothing and possessions generally, as well as many other activities involved in looking after people's physical needs and well-being. The emotional caring activities involve nurturing, supporting, mediating, comforting, tending and bolstering. Gillian Pascall (1986) says 'in simple terms, caring is looking after people'. Women are brought up to believe that caring for others is a fundamental part of their existence as women. They are taught (and see it as their function) to care for children, men, and the sick, elderly and disabled dependants in the family, and therefore, by extension, in the community. It is often assumed that this is a natural part of being a woman and is based on the fact that women give birth and nurture their babies. Gillian Pascall says that such assumptions are unquestioned by the social scientists and politicians who develop theories and social policies, as well as by the women who do the caring. Vivien Nice (1988) jokes seriously that some of the 'evidence' for this is based on work done on rats! Gillian Dalley (1988) points out that there is a confusion here between such differences in women and men being based on nature rather than on social factors. Janet Finch and Dulcie Groves (1983) discuss the idea that 'caring is the concept which marks the boundary between "being" and "doing"'. By this they mean that women are essentially passive, and express their femininity through their caring natures. Conversely, men tend to be active in the world outside the family and express themselves through their careers, that is, by what they 'do'. But the 'doing' nature of caring should not be underestimated. Caring is 'doing', as anyone looking after someone else can vouchsafe, but it is so undervalued that what is meant by men 'doing' in the world outside the family is that they are in control and often making decisions for women as well as for themselves. 'Caring for' someone (tending another person) is not the same as 'caring about' someone (feeling for another person). Caring for someone involves physical and emotional 'doing' and support for that person. Gillian Dalley (1988) says that these two aspects of caring come together particularly in motherhood, so remain separate for men, who rarely get involved in the 'caring for' part. Jalna Hanmer and Daphne Statham (1988) point out that there are definite and clear social and psychological criteria by which women are judged as mothers.

If women do not do the caring directly, then they are responsible for arranging for it to be done by other women such as cleaners and nannies. There is a class as well as a gender issue here, in that the lower the class to which a woman belongs, the more intimate the caring tasks she will be doing directly, either for her family, or as low-paid worker in the personal social services. Conversely, the higher the class to which a woman belongs, the more likely it is that she will have someone doing these tasks for her and so be one removed from them, although still held to be responsible for them. The main reward offered for domestic caring is the personal 'fulfilment' that 'caring for' is supposed to, and can, give. There can be real satisfaction obtained from looking after someone in a loving way but without denying one's own needs or undervaluing what is being done. The problem for women is that, as Jean Baker Miller (1988) says, women are encouraged to transform their needs as if they were identical to those of others.

The government's policy of caring for people in the community rather than in institutions, that is, 'community care' (HMSO 1989) depends on women's willingness to offer free caring. As fewer state services are provided for those people who cannot look after themselves, if they cannot pay for privatised services they have to depend on unpaid relatives and friends (mostly women) to care for them. Such women are expected to 'cope' and are largely left alone to care for others without support. Those men who do get involved with caring for someone else, usually single fathers or partners of elderly women, get far more help and support, from neighbours, family and social services. This is based on assumptions in our culture that men should be in paid work and that they are not really capable unaided of domestic work.

Caring skills are undervalued, taken for granted and exploited. Although women often gain satisfaction from caring for others, at the same time they can feel, and are, in fact, undervalued, powerless, and lacking in self esteem. Carers may face abuse from those for whom they are caring. This happens particularly to black women carers, for example in homes for elderly people, but can also be part of being exploited as a carer, as a daughter by an elderly mother, a wife by a husband, or care staff by the clients and the agency employing them.

As long as they are reasonably fit and healthy, women do not expect other people to care for them in the same way as they care for others and as men usually expect to be cared for. In fact, many women find it difficult to accept care from others or ask for it even if they do need it.

Because women do not expect to be cared for, they generally learn to care for themselves – up to a point: women look after themselves less well than they look after others, putting their own interests after those of others. They usually provide adequate physical care for themselves, probably because they realise that they cannot care for others unless they themselves are in reasonable health. By contrast, men who are left alone often appear incapable of looking after themselves, probably because they are used to being looked after by others.

When it comes to their own emotional needs, women often find it difficult to take these seriously, partly because they may conflict with the needs of others, but also because to attend to their own needs may attract criticism from others. So, for example, to go all out for a career is considered selfish and unfeminine.

Janet Finch and Dulcie Groves (1983) talk of women having 'a career as carers'. That is, women are seen by men, and see themselves, as bound to a caring role because they are women. It is important to acknowledge the cost to women of caring for others. There are personal costs including the hard, unappealing, never-ending and repetitive work involved, and the effects on other relationships, and on life style. There are costs to health. Research by Ian Sinclair, Roy Parker, Diana Leat and Jenny Williams (1990) on caring for elderly people shows that 'most [carers] do not want their relative to enter residential care, but such a step does, on average, benefit their own mental health'. Janina Surma (1991) highlights the pressures carers face. These include physical exhaustion, mental stress and the breakdown of close relationships. There are, of course, economic and career costs, with women giving up jobs and careers in order to bring up children or care for other dependents, resulting in loss of income and status (Gillian Dalley, 1988; Jalna Hanmer and Daphne Statham, 1988).

Julia Phillipson (1989) concludes that although women know how complex the work of caring is, in our society it is 'relegated to its routine tending components', and it is given insufficient recognition, status and pay. For example, care assistants, home helps, foster parents and child carers (both child minders and nursery workers) are all paid at very low rates. Unpaid carers often exist on allowances which keep them on the 'breadline'.

Why do men not do 'women's work'?

Caring tasks for women involve far more intimate tasks than for men who find themselves in a situation of caring for others. Clare Ungerson (1983) argues that there is a taboo in contemporary Western society about the management of human excreta: 'Is it simply the fact that the job is unpleasant and women carry it out because men have used their power and refused to do it?' Or is there a feeling by men of a 'taboo', a danger of pollution if they transgress intimacy boundaries when caring for others? Jalna Hanmer and Daphne Statham (1988) comment that 'a loss of masculine identity is particularly felt when men cross over into intimate areas of care such as washing and caring for bodies and the cleaning of faeces and human dirt. These activities are core characteristics of caring identified as suitable for women'. Ann Oakley (1974) writes in her research into housework that one of the women she interviewed said that her husband ran out of the room rather than be involved in changing their baby's nappy, because it made him sick (quoted by Clare Ungerson, 1983)

This feeling of a taboo against men doing intimate caring tasks can be almost an excuse for them not to be involved in such work either privately (in the family) or in public (in the personal social services). It is possible that men are not readily expected or required to do such tasks because they know that women will. It is as if there were a conspiracy here, between men putting forward and women accepting the idea that men cannot do these caring tasks and that they are a natural basic aspect of being a women. There is a connection too between this caring role being 'dumped' on to women and the expression of emotion. Expressing emotion is seen as a womanly attribute, whereas manliness is equated with the suppression of emotion (Kenneth More in films about the Second World War, or James Dean in his films, are examples of such 'manliness'). 'Womanly' attributes related to the expression of emotion can be linked to the skills necessary for caring for others, including responsiveness, the capacity to be flexible, and the ability to predict others' needs and responses. Since it is unmanly to express emotion about how he feels, that is, cares about, another person, so it is then also unmanly to 'care for', that is, to tend to the intimate needs of another person.

Men are uncomfortable doing 'women's work', caring for others, so they try to get out of doing it as quickly as possible by saying that they are not naturally good at it like women, and by climbing the career ladder to manage the people who do the caring. They may also feel uncomfortable in caring roles because these roles are considered to be 'sissy' or 'soft' and therefore of low status. This provides an incentive for men to seek promotion out of caring jobs. It is interesting to speculate whether men gravitate towards jobs which are already high status or whether the jobs become high status because they are being done by men (see Cynthia Cockburn, 1988; also Anne Phillips and Barbara Taylor, 1980).

Women's work

Women's caring skills are often a way into paid employment. Most 'women's work' involves direct caring or support for others, that is, the ten deadly 'C'-type jobs (catering, cleaning, clerking, cashiering, counter minding, clothes making, clothes washing, coiffuring, child minding, and care of the frail and needy). Caring is seen as an activity which takes place outside the mainstream commercial and industrial activity of society. All caring jobs are badly paid and have low status (Rosalyn Baxandall, Elizabeth Ewen, and Linda Gordon, 1976).

Michael Webb (in Ivan Reid and Eileen Wormald, 1982) analyses the research into gender differences in the labour market, which confirms that women are poorly represented in the higher-paid and higher-status jobs. Most airline pilots and surgeons (very high status jobs) are men, while most air stewardesses and nurses (lower status 'service' jobs) are women. One study of clerical workers (M. Benet, 1972) demonstrated that women receive 20 to 50 per cent less office space than men doing roughly the same work in the same office, and that the higher the concentration of women in a particular area of the office, the lower the standard of decor. Women have less chance of promotion and training and are more likely to be unemployed: 'While marriage may give a man an unpaid helpmate, it often gives a woman responsibi-lities that restrict her in the labour market'. He concludes that segregation between the sexes at work has not significantly altered. H. Wainwright (1978) calls the different roles within the world of work (as well as within wider society) that women and men occupy, 'industrial apartheid'. Angela Coyle and Jane Skinner (1988) say that 'it is the combination of occupational segregation and part time working which has enabled women's pay to be determined at levels significantly lower than men's'. In 1990, women's gross full-time weekly earnings were still only 77 per cent of men's (EOC, 1991).

Most women do not join unions, and those unions representing 'women's work' tend to be weak. Compare, for example, the Union for Shop, Distributive, and Allied Workers (USDAW), which has mainly women members, with the Transport and General Workers' Union (TGWU) which represents mainly men.

Within the world of paid work, the gender stereotyping of men and women is very apparent. Women not only do the direct caring work, but also service men in their jobs. As receptionists, secretaries, administrative and clerical assistants, nurses and social workers, women 'care for' men at work, mimicking domestic relationships. In the private sector it is taken for granted that a good personal assistant will 'look after' her boss. She will make tea for him and his guests, remember his important anniversary dates, buy the necessary cards and presents for him, book his holidays, even buy his cigarettes and cover for his mistakes. Secretaries to women bosses are far less likely to 'service' them in this way.

Women's work in the personal social services

The very structure of the personal social services highlights and underpins the role of women as carers. This is true both in field social work and in residential and day care practice. The personal social services provide a stark example of the way in which women tend to be confined to low-status care and support jobs at work. It is assumed that they know 'naturally' how to work with clients, as this is seen as work that every woman can do 'instinctively' as an extension of childbearing and childcare.

Black women in the personal social services suffer disadvantages experienced by black people generally and by all women (Isabella Stone, 1988, and SSI, 1991). They suffer double prejudice in that they are discriminated against by both white men and women as black people, and also by men as black women. They are seen therefore principally as servers and carers in their paid jobs, even more than white women. In the personal social services they find themselves in the majority as care assistants in residential establishments in cities, in the lowest-status, worst-paid jobs, involving the most intimate caring tasks and with the least prospects of promotion. Bandana Ahmad (1990) makes a distinction between black workers and black professional workers: 'Black workers' invisibility has not been so much due to their absence, but because of their employment status'. She says that Black manual and non professional workers have always been in the caring services, but now 'debates and arguments about recruiting more "Black workers to meet the needs of Black clients" have somehow ignored this Black "manual and non professional" presence who are workers as well. So it seems that when we refer to Black workers in caring services, we mean Black "professionals"'.

Lesbian carers are also discriminated against on account of their sexuality. It is often assumed that gay and lesbian carers are more likely than heterosexuals to abuse their professional roles. There is still tremendous prejudice against non-heterosexual people fostering or adopting children and working in children's homes. This is based both on a false belief that gay men are paedophiles and also that children will be given undesirable role models by lesbian and gay carers. In 1991 a lesbian couple approved by the local authority as adopters had the child removed by a court after a great deal of public pressure against them (*The Daily Telegraph*, 23 January 1991).

David Howe (1986) refers to the 'vertical' segregation of women, where they remain in lower-status jobs. He also discusses what he calls 'horizontal' segregation: by this he means the discrimination against women even at the same levels of employment as men in the personal social services hierarchy. When the racial characteristics of female employees are considered, the patterns of work segregation become even more pronounced. His research shows that women social workers are far more likely to have case loads heavily biased towards work with elderly, disabled and mentally ill people. Women predominate throughout all residential work, but particularly in caring for elderly people. This is especially true for black women in urban areas. The important point here is that these client groups are of low status even within the caring professions, so they are of no interest to male social workers. He concludes, 'Certain types of work, particularly those with a high grading, are seen as "suitable" for men.'

Vivien Nice (1988) says that it is their caring role and 'concern with others that has led to the growth of a workforce of largely female social workers, and which keeps many of those social workers at the service delivery end of the hierarchy'.

Gender and work

It is still very hard for people to work in areas which are traditionally considered to be 'suitable' for the opposite sex. So, for example, a man wishing to care for children is considered to be a 'sissy'; women fire-fighters have been rejected and treated badly by their male colleagues.

Sometimes the name of a job is changed to make a woman's job more acceptable for a man, for example, charge nurse instead of sister, or officer in charge instead of house mother. People make negative career choices in order not to be in a job that is considered unsuitable for their gender. Women often do not consider management jobs. Men in caring jobs usually try to gain quick promotion to management posts, which they find more comfortable. This process is fostered and encouraged by doubts being cast (both by men and some women) on the femininity of 'career' women. The more successful a woman becomes in her career, the more doubts are cast on her femininity. Yet, of course, the more successful a man is in a career, the more desirable he becomes as a spouse and father.

These long-held views about what is regarded as 'suitable' work are now being challenged by women. We all grew up in a society where views about work and the role of women are deeply entrenched. These affect us all in our choice of work and attitudes to careers.

Why do women do the caring?

How is the caring role for women both in the home and in paid work propagated from generation to generation? How and why have the biological differences between men and women affected their different roles and positions in society? In other words, why is it that women continue to do the caring? How is it that women find it difficult to develop their potential apart from the caring and nurturing which they do so well and apparently naturally? This has been discussed and analysed elsewhere (Jan Beagley, 1986; Janet Finch and Dulcie Groves, 1983; Gillian Dalley, 1988; and Vivien Nice, 1988).

Here we will look only at those aspects of socialisation that are particularly relevant to this book. We can begin to find answers to these questions in the way in which children are brought up and educated, the expectations of parents, and the influence of the media. In the next chapter we will look also at some of the historical reasons for this situation.

Gender and families

Dorothy Jongeward and Dru Scott (1975) look at the typical 'script' that most women, especially if they are white, learn and internalise as children: 'I am nice and caring, a feeling person'. Black women may also have the additional 'script' that they should serve white people. Black carers are frequently expected to tolerate racism from both colleagues and clients. For example, black staff working with elderly people are exposed to racist remarks on a daily basis. These are regarded by managers as 'part of the job'.

Such messages really distort the unique potential of each woman and set the limits on what women do in their lives. The typical male 'scripts' of being aggressive, stoical and repressing feelings are, of course, just as limiting for them.

Most families and child rearing reinforce gender differences, with girls still being encouraged towards caring tasks and roles, and boys towards the more rational scientific and technical ones. Girls are more likely to be encouraged to stay at home and help their mothers, boys to play with computers, or outside with their friends, and to go to football matches.

Education

Schools also play their part in fostering different behaviour between the sexes (Jane Steedman, 1983). Despite the Sex Discrimination Act, girls are still encouraged to study the arts and domestic and social sciences whilst boys opt for (with encouragement) the sciences, technology and business studies. Chris Mihill (1990) quotes research which shows that primary school boys are 'computer bullies', leaving girls with a hatred of technology: 'Boys dominated the area immediately in front of the keyboard, whereas girls literally sat at the back . . . Computer games are frequently racist, sexist, militaristic and competitive in format, emphasising the joys of technical domination and mastery'. A national survey (Alan Smithers and Pauline Zientek, 1991) shows that five-year-olds in primary school already have very stereotyped views about gender. More than half the children in the survey thought that hairdressing, teaching and looking after sick people was the preserve of women. Fire-fighting, being a scientist, repairing cars and climbing mountains were almost exclusively the province of men. Both boys and girls stated these opinions.

In the decreasing number of single sex girls' schools, girls do better academically and are more likely to take sciences, as they are not compared to boys and not so likely to follow 'feminine' trends. In mixed classes, boys often get more attention from teachers than do girls. American studies suggest that teachers treat girls and boys more differently than they realise (Carol Nagy Jacklyn, 1991). Girls do as well as, if not better than, boys academically up to puberty and then they become aware that it is still considered 'unfeminine' to be too bright, and they tend to start playing down their achievements in order not to be considered 'bluestockings'

(Ann Bone, 1983; Alan Grigg, 1989; Peggy Hollinger, 1991; Jane Steedman, 1983; and Katherine Whitehorn, 1986). The tendency to prefer to do less well than their male peers follows through into adulthood. In dual-career families women are still reluctant to place their careers ahead of those of their partners.

The expectations of parents

Girls are still considered 'catered for' once they marry. A career is often seen to be secondary for women who are married. A colleague of one of the authors once stated that his son was a policeman and his daughter was married. It then came out that in fact she had a managerial post in a bank! Thus it still appears to be the case, that, as George Eliot stated in the nineteenth century, 'We don't ask what a woman does – we ask whom she belongs to' (*The Mill on the Floss*, Everyman, 1974, quoted by Janet Finch and Dulcie Groves, 1983).

Sharon Tolbert-Stroud (in Dorothy Jongeward and Dru Scott, 1979) makes the important point that 'Black families raise their daughters to accept work or a career as a natural part of their lives; work to them, then, is not a liberating goal, but rather a life long imposed necessity.' Black women are therefore often well equipped for the demands of being in paid employment as well as running homes. She continues that black women are often labelled as 'independent, liberated, free thinking, goal orientated, aggressive; yet, in reality, black women are the most powerless group in our society'.

Boys are encouraged and expected to take paid employment more seriously than girls. Despite the fact that most women are in paid employment, contribute to basic household and living expenses and, as we said before, represent 90 per cent of single parents, men are still seen as breadwinners.

The media

The media also play a very important part in this process; from the advertisements featuring women doing the washing and having coffee with other women clearly not in paid employment, and men in business, driving fast cars, and/or with their mates drinking in pubs, to the 'page 3 girls'. (Apart from in the gay media, where are there photographs of nude men?)

The process whereby women continue in their role as carers is to the advantage of men as they are 'cared for', both at home and at work. Women play their part in the continuation of this process through accepting this caring role.

To end this section on a more positive note, we can acknowledge that there have been some changes in gender roles. Factors such as the development of generally available safe contraception and the increased longevity of women have had some influence on making more equal the roles and positions of women and men in society. However, there is still a long way to go before women are in a position to make free choices about what they want to do with their lives.

Issues of care and control in the personal social services

It is significant that although the caring side of social work has recently attracted a good deal of attention from women writers, the control aspect appears to have been largely ignored. Perhaps this is because as an activity largely associated with men it tends to be taken for granted, so there is thought to be no need to examine it.

The emphasis on caring as the main activity involved in the personal social services is misleading on a number of counts.

● Most local authority social work is actively concerned with control as much as with caring. Child care and mental health legislation prescribe the work of social workers.
● Insufficient resources are made available for preventive work, so social workers can easily find themselves confined to a policing role. Only voluntary organisations such as the Family Welfare Association, Family Service

Units, and Relate have a real opportunity to do much therapeutic work. Also, many experienced practitioners are leaving the statutory services in order to do 'real' social work.

● The caring aspect of social work has been largely relegated to residential work and home care. Even here, care staff still face restrictions against becoming involved with clients on an emotional level. They tend to be categorised as manual workers, and rarely hold a professional social work qualification. This means that they are not seen as able to do therapeutic work and also that if they spend time talking to residents this is secondary to their 'proper' tasks of physical caring.

● The probation service, which has traditionally been regarded as having a good balance between the caring and control aspects of social work, periodically comes under pressure to become more identified with law and order.

● Good quality care surely involves control but not of the abusive or punitive variety. Like all children, those in care need to be controlled by boundaries being set on their behaviour. Everybody needs boundaries, but some people need these set from outside if, for whatever reason such as learning difficulties, old age, or mental health problems they are unable to set their own. As well as setting boundaries for the person being cared for, it is important that carers set boundaries for themselves. This enables them to empower the person being cared for to be as independent as possible, rather than that person being deprived of any power that it is possible to maintain or achieve.

● Even though a culture of caring is encouraged at the practice end of the personal social services, the culture of management is one of control. Care and control, although often referred to together, sit uneasily with each other and have done so through most of social work history. We shall be exploring these points subsequently. The fact that women are regarded as carers serves to reinforce the split and is reflected in the various branches of the personal social services.

Male and female dominated areas of the work in the personal social services

The controlling function of social caring has historically tended to attract men whilst women are usually more comfortable in caring roles. Many women decide to become social workers because they believe the advertisements that working in the personal social services is to do with caring. They are not aware of, and are uncomfortable with, the control part of the work with which they then find themselves involved. Many men are attracted to the control aspects of social work, including management, but are insufficiently in touch with its caring components. Women managers bring a caring component to the harsh world of management, which serves to provide a link and support to the caring activities central to the personal social services. Although women occupy most of the caring jobs in the personal social services, there are some fields where there is a clear gender split.

The main examples of these are hospital social work, day nurseries, residential care (particularly for elderly people), occupational therapy, and home help services, where mainly women are employed, and penal establishments where many men are employed.

Hospital social work

Hospital social work has developed from the lady almoner system. Ronald Walton (1975) comments that although men were eligible to train as almoners from 1919, there is no mention of any man doing so. Jan Beagley (1986) says that the profession of medical social work is an outstanding example of a service almost completely devised and dominated by women. But although the majority of hospital social workers are women, their managers are mainly men. Hospital social workers usually operate as part of medical 'firms' rather than as part of the social work team as the first priority. So even though they may be aware of being part of the social work team, and of the wider social services or social work department, most hospital social workers are attached to a particular ward or wards, and to a specific medical 'firm', under a consultant. They therefore automatically feel first and foremost to be a part of this group. The consultant is usually a man, as are the other doctors. The nurses, the paramedical people, including the social workers, in the 'firm' – those people doing the basic caring tasks – will be mainly women. The doctors (the men) clearly are in control, making most of the decisions, including non-medical ones relating to clients, such as when and how a patient is discharged.

Any social worker who queries such a decision, for social reasons, often has to fight to get her view known, accepted or even heard by the doctors. The non-medical staff (the women), carry out these decisions. There is very clearly in most hospitals a hierarchy, with doctors (mainly men and often white), at the top, and nurses, auxiliaries and cleaners (almost all female and often black), at the bottom. Social workers fit in somewhere around the nurses in status. Thus men are typically in control, making decisions, and women are responding to the men's requirements and orders, while providing the caring service to clients where women are in the majority.

Hospital social workers are not seen as professional people, on a par with doctors, in terms of making professional decisions and assessments. Professional and gender issues come together here in that social work (particularly in hospitals) is seen as the 'hand maiden' of medicine, with women doing the bidding of men and in the caring role, with relatively low status.

Nursery work, residential day care, and care in the community services

These areas of work are seen traditionally as basically caring jobs, so women are employed in them, and they are considered to be of low status. Nursery workers, day centre staff, care assistants, home helps and occupational therapists are seen as doing practical caring tasks rather than as professionals doing highly skilled work with vulnerable groups of people. To look after groups of under-fives with severe social problems so that their emotional and intellectual as well as physical needs are met, and also working with their families, requires skills of the highest order. Yet nurseries are staffed almost exclusively by women who are predominantly young and inexperienced (SSI, 1991).

The situation is similar for staff such as care assistants in homes for elderly people. Here casework, group work, bereavement counselling, family therapy and nursing skills are necessary. Yet such work is also accorded very low status, being seen as manual work rather than as a skilled job with vulnerable people.

There is insufficient professional training for people working in these areas. Such jobs, because of their low status, are often held by black women. It is interesting to surmise that if more men did this work (usually residential homes for elderly people will have perhaps only one or two male care assistants, to help with the lifting, or with any male clients who want a man to help with particular physical tasks), then it would have higher status and be seen in more professional and proactive terms. Indeed in the 1970s social work as a profession wanted to attract more men in order to raise its status.

Figures from individual local authorities suggest that between three-quarters and seven-eighths of day centre staff are women. An overall picture emerges of mostly women working in lower grades, and with men holding a disproportionate number of more senior jobs (SSI, 1991).

Occupational therapists have been employed in increasing numbers in Social Services Departments since the early 1970s. Again, they are predominantly young female staff. Their skills are not recognised and there are poor promotional opportunities for them (SSI, 1991).

Home helps too are mainly women. They have a high degree of responsibility in giving personal support and assessing the significance of changes in their clients' situations. Ian Sinclair, Roy Parker, Diana Leat and Jenny Williams (1990) point out that 'By far the most important domiciliary service in terms of its coverage is home help. This service assists more people than any other branch of the personal social services'. However, home helps work in isolation, getting very little support from colleagues or supervision from managers. They are almost always graded as manual workers and low paid (SSI, 1991). The issue here is that 'caring' is all too often seen in terms of physical caring that can be done by anyone (certainly by any woman automatically), rather than as a part of social work, with professional skills.

A recent study (Jean Spence and Muriel Sawbridge, 1991) found that women community workers were usually identified by managers and colleagues as being responsible for working with girls and women. Such activites are often regarded by men and management as marginal.

The Wagner Committee Report (G. Wagner, 1988) says that caring is seen as unskilled and particularly suitable for women, consistent with their traditional roles, and less appropriate for men (quoted in SSI, 1991). This does not prevent men from being in charge of and managing the services mentioned above.

The penal system

One of the few services that is male-dominated is that of penal and remand establishments. Here the emphasis is clearly on control rather than caring. The exceptions are the establishments for women where women officers are often seen as doing a 'man's' job, controlling criminals.

It is very noticeable that prison officers are accorded higher status than are care staff for other groups of people. They are trained before starting their jobs, there is a proper career structure, and a strong, effective union. None of these is true for people working in other residential settings.

It is worth noting that prison officers do not have to do the day-to-day caring and running of the penal establishment, since this is done by the residents. The prison staff have the task of supervising these functions. This is different from the staff in other types of residential establishment (homes for children, adults and elderly people who cannot live on their own) whose main function is seen as caring for the residents on a practical and emotional level. In practice there is often a high level of subtle control, for example inflexible daily routines, lack of choice, and a lack of consultation and of personal possessions (London Borough of Camden, 1987; Tim Booth, 1987). Control which is not so subtle but veers towards abuse also occurs, such as 'pindown' techniques (Allan Levy, 1991).

Women prison officers are seen as not fulfilling the conventional feminine stereotype. They are regarded as 'butch', as masculine; in other words, as not 'real' or 'proper' women. Women social care practitioners often experience a dilemma of how to deal with the power they hold over clients.

The most obviously male dominated area of social work is that of management, particularly senior management. Men as managers, have control over resources, including women workers. We shall return to this theme in Chapter 4.

In this chapter we have seen how personal social services organisations promote a philosophy of caring.

We have examined the meaning of caring and why it is that in our society women are expected to take responsibility for it, not only in the home, but also in paid work settings.

The vast majority of caring and support roles in the workplace are held by women and have come to be known as 'women's work'. Most of the work in the personal social services is of this nature.

We noticed that the caring philosophy promoted by the personal social services is only one side of the story. A great deal of this work consists of control functions, for example statutory work occupies a high proportion of social worker time. There tends to be a gender split between the caring aspects, which are overwhelmingly carried out by women, and the controlling aspects of the work, which appear to attract men.

3

Our Inheritance: The History of Women's Work in the Personal Social Services

In this chapter we trace the history of women's work in the personal social services and the way in which the care and control aspects have become polarised over the course of time. The historical background helps us to understand why women are still doing the caring jobs and men are still holding control of management. This is in spite of the position of women changing towards equality with that of men through battles (particularly in this century) for equal rights and equal opportunities.

Women's role in the home

Women through the ages have been the procreators, nurturers and carers. Most of us are taught to accept as fact that at the beginning of civilization as we know it, when humans settled in caves, men would go out hunting, leaving women behind to care for the children. However this is now being questioned by feminist historians (Rosalind Miles, 1989). Also the matriarchal cult of the goddess in prehistoric times should not be forgotten (George Frankl, 1989). Later, as civilisation progressed, both men and women worked the land. Women at the same time were also concerned with feeding and clothing the family: spinning, weaving, tending the weak and frail members, educating and training the children and running the house. Thus there were already differences in the roles of men and women, in that men worked the land and women were more involved with the domestic animals, and chores about the house. Of course, they were involved with childbearing and child rearing for most of their adult lives. Childbearing was of great importance to keep up the stock of human beings, when life expectancy was very low and child mortality very high.

Men were able to hold power at all levels because they were free of childbearing and child rearing responsibilities and so available to participate in social and political life. With the coming of industrialisation and the rise of capitalism in the nineteenth century, paid work gradually became even more separate from home. Men increasingly worked in factories, mines, dockyards and mills to earn money rather than on their own land, or plying their own craft. This exaggerated the tendency for the domestic side of life to be left to women. Paid work started to become separate from leisure or private work. Pre-industrial people worked for money or its equivalent, but this was for themselves and their families, done on a co-operative basis within the family or small local community. Later, as industrialisation developed and more labour was needed, working-class women (and children too) did go out to work in factories, but only in the most menial jobs. They were considered and treated more or less as animals: we have all heard about pregnant women working in mines, pulling carts of coals on all fours. However, they were still also responsible for keeping the home and the family going. These women, it would seem, had it badly both ways: they were still involved with their child rearing and general caring tasks at home, while also doing the worst-paid jobs in mines and factories.

Upper- and middle-class women of this time had a very different way of life. They were not expected to care for the children they produced, nor to undertake any domestic or paid work outside the home. They had servants, governesses, and boarding schools to take care of all this for them. The men of the house: the father, husband or sometimes brother (like Mr and Miss Murdstone in Charles Dickens' *David Copperfield*, 1986) were out all day, making money, running factories and shops. These men were very much in charge and in control of society's, their own and their family's destinies. The women were legally the property of the men, to be dealt with as such, and with little power and say over their lives. They were expected to be the 'angel' of the house that their men retreated to from the hurly-burly and bustle of the world outside. They were to be shown off as possessions demonstrating the success and status of the men through the women's good (submissive) behaviour and the finery that they wore. (For a Marxist analysis of this patriarchal social structure, see Judy Lown in Eva Gamarnikow *et al.* (eds) 1983). There were, of course, exceptions to this, like Octavia Hill and Florence Nightingale. However, these women had to forgo family life and having children, but they were still involved in caring work. Margaret Forster in *Significant Sisters* (1986) writes about such women. She says that they were the initiators and leaders of change to more equal opportunities for women.

The work of the American artist Judy Chicago (a reconstruction of an enormous dinner table with the place settings labelled with the names of significant women through the ages) shows just how many women have had real influence on science, medicine and the arts. These women should not be lost sight of. There seems to be something like a conspiracy by white men to ignore these women, similar to the way significant black people (such as Mary Seacole in the Crimean War) are also denied their true status, place and acknowledgement in Western history.

The process of industrialisation really only confirmed and accentuated the fact that throughout history women in general have been dismissed as second class citizens, with no power, rights or control over their lives, and relegated to low status work.

Moving into paid work

The First World War changed the whole concept of 'women's work' and created new opportunities for women (Ronald Walton, 1975). Because large numbers of men were away fighting or had been killed, women took over many of their jobs, particularly in factories. This, together with the suffragette movement for votes for women, really affected the position of women in relation to paid work. After the war, women continued the process of moving into jobs previously closed to them. Nancy Astor became the first woman MP to take a seat in Parliament, the Sex Disqualifications (Removals) Act (1919) opened higher appointments in the Civil Service to women, Oxford University admitted women, and the first women magistrates were appointed in 1920 (Ronald Walton, 1975). However, women were at the same time still doing the caring at home and the low-paid jobs outside. So this development was hard on individual women who were trying to run their homes as before and work outside too.

During the Second World War when men were away fighting, women again took over their civilian jobs. Women were also more involved with the war itself than in the First World War, both in the women's armed forces and in the 'war work' in armament factories. They were supported by a network of nurseries to care for their children (see Chapter 6).

Since the Second World War, women have continued to work in all types of jobs, but the fact that they are also still held responsible for housework and child care is being increasingly questioned, with an expectation developing that men should participate in the domestic chores. However, the problem has remained of women doing low-status low-paid 'women's work'. In the 1950s and 1960s more women began to move into certain careers associated with 'women's work' such as nursing, teaching and social work. Ronald Walton (1975) says that there was a gradual trend for women to move into a widening range of occupations including the higher professions such as architecture and accountancy. But they often had to choose between a career and a family. Some organisations did not allow women to continue working after they were married or when they became pregnant. Most women would work only until they married and had a family, so would not bother with further or higher education or to develop their careers. Only the women who remained single would continue with their education and have careers. Since the 1970s women have succeeded in combining careers with cleaners and nannies) and are moving into male-dominated professions such as law, industry and commerce, but are still not well represented in the more senior posts.

Women as social carers

If a historical perspective is taken on the controlling and caring 'strands' of social welfare, it becomes clear that the position of women as social carers stems from the domestic and public position of women and men, on which the origins of public welfare were based.

The Poor Law was an early organised way in which people were looked after when they could not care for themselves, either for a limited period, or for a lifetime, and had no close family or relatives to support them. The Church was responsible for such caring. The Poor Law arose in order to control the movement of needy people from one parish to another, from the territory of one church to another.

In the Jewish and Christian faiths, there has always been an ethic of helping those less fortunate than oneself. However, with the growth of the Protestant ethic within Christianity, helping others became more complex.

Work was thought of as good in itself, which meant that good people who worked hard did well materially, almost a mark of God's approval. However, they were not allowed to participate in 'wild' living and self-indulgence, so some of the excess wealth would be given to others less fortunate than themselves. Only those people considered to be 'deserving' of such help would receive donations. These were people who could not work through perhaps infirmity or old age. Anyone, particularly men, who was able bodied would be deemed fit to work. Anyone able bodied and not working would be dismissed as lazy and feckless and so not deserving of any charity. Help would be given to family men who were too ill to work, and to families with no breadwinner: the widows and orphans. No return except gratitude was expected for this material help (in this life at least). This was a way of controlling poor people to avoid the risk of revolution.

With the coming of the Industrial Revolution, the necessity for social care increased very suddenly. People could not always get work and often they would have to move to find it, breaking up family and community networks which previously had provided informal mutual help and support. Thus social work as we know it today began to develop. The well-meaning middle-class woman, with time on her hands, would go to the poor with material help such as food and clothing but also trying to spread ideas about Christian virtue and family life such as that cleanliness is next to Godliness, and that men should be in paid work, and women in the home servicing the family. Chris Rojak *et al.* (1988) make the point that perhaps both the middle-class women doing their 'good works' and the recipients of such help were sowing the seeds of further female oppression 'by colluding with a system of help that sanctified womanly attributes as ideal for care provision and identified women as the clients needing help, rather than identifying the structural weaknesses of the social system causing problems'. They also say that the class factor inherent in these early social work relationships undermined any potential unity between women. On the other hand, the moral welfare movement of this time played an important role in protecting young women from male exploitation: in attempting, for example, to stop men from using teenage women as prostitutes (Sheila Jeffreys, 1985). There was a strong Christian impetus behind this work.

The early women 'case workers' would go and talk to working-class and 'fallen' women to try and convince them to live Christian lives. So prostitutes and women who had illegitimate children, for example, were urged to mend their sexual ways. There was one set of sexual standards for men and another for women. This double standard of sexual morality to some extent still exists today. For example, a young woman in care is considered to be in moral danger if she is sexually active, whereas a young man in a similar situation is not judged by the same criteria.

The origins of the personal social services at the end of the nineteenth century were based on this charitable tradition of middle-class people who were good practising Christians and successful at business, giving to the poor and needy. It was the men who set up, ran and controlled the charities, while women propagated the middle-class Christian values among working-class people by visiting their homes.

Thus the caring side of social work originated from middle-class women going out to help others. The controlling aspect to this early welfare work appeared when these first social workers felt that they had to save the souls of the 'fallen' and working-class people they were helping. Help would be given only if the recipients were considered to be 'deserving'; that is, if they accepted the moral precepts which were imposed on them. The Charity Organisation Society (the COS) represented this controlling 'strand'. It developed to bring together all the different helping organisations, philanthropic and religious, and to co-ordinate their functions. It was a public body and so a male domain. (The only woman member of its council was Octavia Hill.) Men had control over the money that was given out to the poor and needy. However, its main task and area of control became to decide on who needed what help; to separate out those 'deserving' of help from those 'undeserving'. Here we have the beginnings of the social work 'interview', 'case work', 'assessment' and 'care planning'. This was linked to social policy, religious moral codes and public spending, over which women had no influence. These were considered to be 'male' matters, even though it was women who were the main recipients of welfare and it was women who did the caring. Despite this gender separation it was perhaps the only time in the history of social work that the care and control elements existed together in a degree of harmony from the point of view of those offering the service.

Residential work

Residential work goes back very far in the history of social work. Workhouses for those people who could not look after themselves and who had no one to help them were established as part of the Poor Law. These were run by men (the controlling aspect of welfare), but with women doing the actual day-to-day work. Men, women and children were kept separate even if they belonged to the same family. Conditions were horrifying, to discourage people in need from entering these establishments if they could find care for themselves in the wider community. There was an expectation that the residents should be grateful and submissive for the 'charity' they were receiving.

There have also always been asylums and prisons for 'lunatics' and 'criminals'. More women ended up in the former and more men in the latter places. These places also had appalling conditions, with containment rather than care being the main objective. There is a legacy of many such psychiatric and penal establishments built in Victorian times. They were very large, imposing buildings built away from towns and with security as their main feature. Leonard Davis (1982) says 'Residential care has always been about living in large buildings'. He looks also at the other historical aspects of residential care: that establishments were single sex; and that titles for staff such as 'matron', 'warden', 'superintendent' 'officer in charge' used within residential care emphasised its controlling aspect as well as the dependency and inadequacy of the residents. There were rigid daily routines, rigid times for visiting, and excessive corporal punishment.

Residential work was largely ignored when social work was developing as a profession; it has always been seen as a last resort – to control someone – rather than as an area with potential for positive work with clients. Eric Sainsbury (1977) says 'Institutional life may intensify divisions between the needs of the staff (for a quiet life) and the needs of residents, which in turn lead to the formulation of rules or to the imposition of subtle emotional and moral pressures'. Mostly women were (and still are) employed in residential establishments (with men in control as 'superintendents' or 'officers in charge'). These women were largely untrained and unqualified, it being thought that such work was merely an extension of 'women's work' at home. Hugh Barr (1987) says that the Seebohm report (F. Seebohm, 1968) says little about residential work as its emphasis was on the development of field services. 'Advocates of a better deal for residential work feared that it was being cast in the shadows'. The Seebohm report eclipsed the Williams report (L. Williams, 1967) on residential care just as two decades later, similarly the

Griffiths report (R. Griffiths, 1989) and the government White Paper stemming from it (HMSO, 1989) on care in the community has overshadowed the Wagner report (1988) on residential care.

However, the Wagner report is part of a process whereby residential work is being seen as a significant part of social work generally, as part of a profession with its own body of theories (about institutionalisation, for example) and standards of care and practice. At the same time residential work is being privatised, with residential establishments being sold off by local authority Social Services Departments. This could easily become a regressive step, with insufficient salaries, and the status and training of mostly women staff deteriorating even further. It is not generally recognised that working in residential settings requires skill and knowledge far beyond just the physical caring for someone else. Residential living should be a positive choice for clients, and residential social work should be a positive career option for both women and men and not just an extension of 'women's work'.

Developing social theory

Between the two world wars, the Poor Law was finally technically demolished, and some welfare rights were developed. But these welfare rights were based on the needs of working men and their families, if these men for reasons of ill health or injury could no longer either temporarily or permanently continue to work in paid employment. Women had no welfare rights for themselves, but only as dependents of men in paid employment. These public welfare Acts of Parliament were thought out and put into effect by men, since there were no women in Parliament at this time (the end of the nineteenth century and beginning of the twentieth). Even now there is only a minute proportion of women MPs.

Social caring in the 1920s and 1930s first in the USA and then in Britain, adapted theories from Sigmund Freud, and started to analyse in psychological terms the reasons for people being deserving or not of social assistance. Freud was of the opinion that women were lesser beings than men because they lacked something, namely a penis, and he denied their specific psychological development.

This had a long-term influence on psychiatry and social work, which until recently has completely ignored the particular needs of women, and was concerned to help them to become more 'feminine' or adapt to their role in society, that is to 'women's work'. Nevertheless these theories have led to a more caring service from the point of view of non-judgemental attitudes.

During the late 1940s, the concept evolved of the 'problem family', where it was noticed that problems or deviant behaviour manifested by children in some families were related to the relationship issues between the parents (in turn a result of their own upbringing), and between the parents and the children. However the gender roles in the family were not questioned. It was taken for granted that women were at home producing and caring for the children. Women were taught by social workers to cook and sew, and they were helped to look after their families 'properly'. Eve Brook and Ann Davis (1985) call this a 'cosy vision of state provision supporting family life'. But it can also be regarded as a subtle form of social control. It was assumed that men were out in paid employment earning the money to keep their families. Social work for them was help in getting a job. When one of the authors started work as a probation officer in the 1960s in her office in central London, although things were beginning to change, men officers still dealt with men clients, which meant mainly helping them to find work, and women probation officers dealt with women clients, mainly helping them to develop moral values (that is, not to sleep around) and to 'settle down' in conventional family situations. Chris Rojak *et al.* say that the subsequent establishment of the Children's Departments was a doubly oppressing factor for women: 'Firstly, it emphasised women's role with children: women were thought to be the right and best people to provide child care. Secondly, it created "an increase in concern over the training and status of social workers". This in turn led to the development of hierarchical and bureaucratic structures to support the delivery of welfare services, the creation of managerial posts, and consequently better career prospects and salaries. So social work, particularly its managerial or controlling aspects, became increasingly attractive as an occupation for men whilst women were still relegated to the caring jobs.'

Gender and race discrimination

With the development in the 1960s and 1970s of radical social work ideas social work practice and the values on which it is based, did shift to some extent but not in terms of gender. (See Roy Bailey and Mike Brake, 1977; Steve Bolger *et al.*, 1981; Paul Corrigan and Peter Leonard, 1979; and Daphne Statham, 1978.) Chris Rojak *et al.* (1980) say that the significant feminist contribution to social work and policy theory had little effect on practice. (See also Elizabeth Wilson, 1977; Eve Brook and Ann Davis, 1985; Jennifer Dale and Peggy Foster, 1986; Helen Marchant and Betty Wearing, 1986; and Diane Burden and Naomi Gottlieb, 1987.) Although the women's liberation movement was developing powerfully during the 1970s, the personal social services did not take account of its implications. The radical literature of the time saw the contradictions inherent in the structure of social caring, that is, in the welfare state, in class rather than gender terms. Social workers were seen as representatives of an oppressive, middle-class, capitalist-dominated state apparatus controlling the working class. There seemed no way of being a statutory social worker and not being part of this oppressive process. A large number of social work texts produced at that time were written from a socialist, politically radical stance, and all too few grasped the issues about gender, sexuality and race in social work. The fact that men were in control of social work agencies and women were still doing the caring jobs was largely ignored. Ronald Walton (1975) says that the lack of involvement of social work with the women's rights movement at that time is in contrast to the position before the First World War where at least many women social workers were conscious of the need to think through their position on questions of women's suffrage. However, feminist ideas have had an influence on some areas of social work; for example, social work with child abuse (particularly child sexual abuse) and violence to women (see Chapter 9).

There was also at this time a lack of awareness of race issues. There was no understanding of the social and political reasons for the over-representation of black children in care and in special schools, of black people in prisons, and sectioned under mental health legislation. There was no acknowledgement of the role that a dominant white racist society might have in these situations. There were unquestioned assumptions that black families were less stable than white, a higher proportion of black than white children were less intelligent or showed behaviourial and emotional problems, that black people (youths in particular) were more inclined to crime than were white, and that black people (particularly women) were unstable and tended towards mental illness. Since then, even if the situation has not changed sufficiently in that these assumptions are still rife, at least they are being questioned and challenged and the pervasive effects of racism beginning to be recognised. Women from Afro-Caribbean countries were recruited in the 1950s to ease the shortage of nurses in this country. Black women are still being actively recruited but now as social workers, care assistants, nursery workers and child minders by inner city local authorities to deal with black families or children who are regarded by them as 'problems'. This is just a continuation of the process of discrimination against black people by the very process of labelling their families as 'problem' if they do not conform to white middle-class norms. The Kilbrandon (1964) and Seebohm (1968) reports did little to affect the balance of power between men and women in the personal social services. In fact, matters became worse because the considerable increase in numbers of managers in the new Social Service Departments were nearly all men, leaving them still very much in control of a service provided mainly by and for women (see Chapter 4).

An important change affecting social work services in the 1960s were new laws concerned with equal rights. There were four main areas of equal rights addressed in the 1960s, culminating in four relevant laws in the 1970s. The four new Acts were, in chronological order, the Equal Pay Act (1970);

The Rehabilitation of Offenders Act (1974); The Sex Discrimination Act (1975); and the Race Relations Act (1976). (The Chronically Sick and Disabled Persons Act was passed in 1958.)

Local authorities started in the late 1970s to develop equal opportunities policies but in insufficient detail, and with no real strategies. The power structure remained unchanged and based on gender (as well as class, race and disability) discrimination. There was very little development in this area during the 1970s and the 1980s, particularly with the attitude of the government of the time to gender issues, the family and to gay rights. Thatcherism, with its emphasis on the enterprise culture and cuts in public expenditure, had the effect of diminishing the caring culture and engendering more punitive attitudes.

This chapter has looked at the history of 'women's work' and how women's roles in the home has influenced the kinds of jobs which were thought to be suitable for them. Even though their role in the world of paid work has expanded greatly, women are still largely excluded from the most prestigious jobs, that is, senior management posts.

We have also traced the history of the care and control strands in the personal social services. The attitudes of the helping professions towards women clients have confirmed them in their traditional role. In all but a few quarters discriminatory attitudes are still rife in the personal social services, despite equal rights legislation and equal opportunities policies.

We have spent some time in Chapters 2 and 3 looking at the historical and social contexts. We shall now move on to look at care and control in management.

4

Care and Control in Management

We started Chapter 2 by reminding ourselves of the very strong association between caring and the personal social services. We noted that caring roles, although central to personal social services work, are devalued: caring skills are thought to come 'naturally' to women; these jobs are clustered at the bottom of the hierarchy and paid at a very low rate.

We also noticed how these 'caring' jobs carry a 'control' element, which tends to be played down by the public face of the personal social services, and attracts criticism from the media in well-publicised child abuse cases.

Management as control

In this chapter we will look at care and control in the personal social services from a different angle. We will see how management has taken on a strong control function to the neglect of caring. This has had the effect of creating a split within the personal social services, between those in caring and support jobs and those in management. It distorts the way in which management is practised and has encouraged the tendency for men to occupy the management jobs.

There is no doubt that traditional models of management were associated with control. The models that have been handed down to us were based on large organisations such as the Church, the armed services and early systems of

41

government, in which representatives of the ruling class tried to keep the masses in order.

Early management theorists at the end of the nineteenth century applied scientific methods to management in order to increase efficiency. For example, Henri Fayol portrayed managerial work as following the rationality of planning, organising and controlling. Frederick Taylor advocated 'keeping subordinates busily engaged on prescribed work, done in a prescribed way and at a prescribed pace' (Norman Cuthbert, 1970). There are still many managers who behave as though workers need to be controlled in such a way. Theories about human relationships gradually percolated through into the practice of management (Charles Handy, 1985), but alongside these there are still plenty of ideas which emphasise a more mechanistic view.

Men, women and management

In the past, it was taken for granted that people in charge of organisations would be men. Only now is there any questioning of the assumption that has held over nearly 2000 years, that bishops should be men. In most countries women can only join the armed services in suppport roles, so there is no question of their being promoted to the rank of general in the army even if they wanted to.

Britain's first woman prime minister was elected as recently as 1979. The 'captains of industry' have always been men. The vast majority of managerial posts in every sector of employment are held by men. 'Women hold a minuscule twenty-eight main board appointments in the U.K.'s top two hundred companies.' (Lesley Abdela, 1991).

We saw in the last chapter that even in the personal social services, where women have always done most of the face-to-face work with consumers, men have always been in charge of the organisations in which they work. Until very recently women were almost entirely confined to caring roles. Two factors have influenced this state of affairs: social change and the way in which the task of management has been defined.

During the past fifty years, women have increasingly taken on paid jobs. This has coincided with a greater proportion of women going into further and higher education. At least in theory, women are now more available and qualified to take on a wider variety of work, even if social attitudes still stand in their way.

Traditionally, as we have seen, the task of management has been defined in terms of control. This is interesting because the word 'management' has two derivations, one related to control, the other to caring (Alistair Mant, 1977). The Italian word *maneggiare*, roughly translated, means controlling things, especially horses. The French word *menager* means careful use, and is connected with housekeeping (see Chapter 8 for further details).

What seems to have happened is that the control aspects of management have taken prominence in the public arena of paid work, and been associated with men, and the caring aspects have been undervalued and relegated to the home and to women. We will be arguing later that both are equally important to management in the personal social services. Over the last fifty years both these aspects have at different times been in evidence, but the control strand has increasingly come into prominence.

The Curtis report (HMSO 1946), which was concerned with the care of children, argued that women were particularly suitable for the job of children's officer. Children's officers were the directors of Children's Departments. These were previously responsible for the children and families aspect of the work of Social Services and Social Work Departments prior to reorganisation of the personal social services. In 1950, 72 per cent of children's officers in England and Wales were women (Municipal Year Book, 1951). The reorganisation of the personal social services (Local Authorities Social Services Act, 1971) and the subsequent reorganisation of local government in 1974 (Local Government Act) decimated the number of women in senior positions. Although children's officers as a group were more likely to be professionally qualified than the welfare officers, who were mostly men, they did not succeed in gaining the majority of directors' posts (Joy Foster, 1987). Only fourteen of the first 174 Directors of Social

Services were women. As Jane Skinner and Celia Robinson (1988) point out, the 'managerialism' of the 1970s 'seemed to mean that men were seen as having the qualities to direct and plan the new social services'. They quote from the Seebohm report (1968) that 'He (the director) must be able to command the confidence of members, to persuade them to provide more resources for the services to maintain a reasonable balance between the demands made on behalf of different groups in the population, and at the same time to stand up for the department'. They comment that 'managerial qualities seem to have been defined in masculine terminology', and it is not, therefore, surprising that mainly men became the new directors.

This process was encouraged by calls for the introduction of business methods into the personal social services. The Seebohm report argued for more efficient management along the lines of business and industrial methods, which had always in the past been identified with men. By the mid-1980s the 'enterprise culture' was in full swing and local government came under intense pressure to become more businesslike under the scrutiny of the Audit Commission and from legislation forcing them to privatise services. This intensified the process of management being identified with masculine qualities.

The implementation of 'Care in the Community' (HMSO, 1989) could become another strand in the masculinisation of management in the personal social services. The budgetary control aspects of future home care management posts, which have traditionally been held by women, may encourage men to apply and be appointed to these posts in greater numbers.

Thus we have a situation where management is defined in 'masculine' terms. This leads people to believe that men have the skills and qualities to be managers, but women do not match up to the blueprint or the image, so men are more likely than women to consider that they have the relevant skills for management posts (Ruth Popplestone, 1979).

However, men and women have different views about the relative importance of skills necesssary for management, and women who become managers also have different priorities.

Ruth Eley (1986) found a clear picture of gender difference in the relative importance which senior social workers (in Liverpool Social Services Department) attach to various aspects of their supervisory role. She found that most of the men in her study stressed the importance of ensuring that statutory responsibilities are carried out, followed by giving practical advice and guidance in handling cases. Most of the women, however, stressed the importance of supporting staff in the stresses of the job, followed by helping staff to prioritise work and manage a case load, and ensuring statutory responsibilities were carried out. In Chapter 8 we will see that women often have a very different style of management from men.

Management training is usually aimed at men and designed to promote the ('masculine') skills thought to be necessary for managers. The few women who gain access to it are likely to find that they are very much in the minority, that the trainers are white men, and that very little attempt is made to make them feel welcome or recognise that their training needs are not identical to those of men. Most of the books about management are written by men, about men's experience, for men. When *Insight*, the now defunct journal for managers in the personal social services, first started, the only photographs it carried were of men. It took letters of complaint from women to change this.

The process of identifying management with 'masculine' skills has had several unfortunate results:

● It has divorced management from caring roles by emphasising values which are seen to be at odds with caring. This has led to people in caring roles feeling as though managers lack respect and understanding, both for users of the service and for their staff
● It has effectively kept women out of management, even though the vast majority of staff and users of the personal social services are women.
● It has distorted the way in which management is practised.
● It causes women's management skills to go unrecognised.

The divorce of management from caring

A vast abyss has developed between workers and management in many personal social services organisations, and this is not just about wages and conditions of work. It is much more to do with a difference in values between those who are in caring roles and those in management about how people, both staff and consumers, should be treated. An example comes from the Spastics Society and concerns perceptions about the way in which redundancies were handled. Twenty staff are reported to have telephoned a help line complaining that they 'felt worried about the consequences of speaking out about management style and about a growing emphasis on business rather than caring values within the society'. The Director of Marketing (!), Richard Brewster, 'dismissed their fears and said this was normal in a large organisation' (Joy Ogden, 1991). Kate Pryde (1991) says that 'the development of a macho management style has contributed to the repression of social work values and passion about social issues . . . I do know that social workers do care but sense that management and procedures limit their abilities to care'.

The personal exposure of social workers and some first line managers in media coverage of successive child abuse tragedies has left social workers feeling unsupported and vulnerable, and has produced hostile attitudes towards managers for their failure to support their staff. The experience of many grass roots workers is that management is more about putting pressure on staff to carry unreasonable workloads than about giving support. A number of authors have drawn attention to the need for supervision and support, particularly workers involved with abused children. Maggie Lancelot (1990[1]) found that all the women social workers she surveyed rated 'supportive' as an important characteristic of a good senior, but only 28 per cent thought that management would rate it important. A NALGO report (1989) found that supervision was a high priority for staff, but that it is generally irregular, often infrequent and sometimes non-existent. Jalna Hanmer and Daphne Statham (1988) found that even when supervision does exist it is often focused on crisis rather on the emotional impact on the worker.

Supervisors often 'cut off from the pain in clients' lives. The worker, unable to share and thereby receive support from her line manager, is left on her own with the loss and grief of her clients'. They view this as an example of management which emphasises control as opposed to development of staff's potential, and consider that it plays a major role in creating job dissatisfaction.

They quote a DHSS report (1986) which concludes that painful events in the lives of clients are not being addressed by practitioners. This is not surprising if supervision also avoids pain. The NALGO report (1989) quoted an example of a team leader who was told to regard supervision as low priority in favour of the high priority restructuring of the department. A team leader writing in *Insight* (Vicki Golding, 1988) speaks of the dilemmas of dealing with pressure: 'I have been living with fear over the past few weeks. This is not the anxiety which comes from child abuse work but is the result of constant pressure which means I am no longer thinking clearly'. She considers that good work requires good support and not being pressured to take on more than she can handle.

> Increasingly it appears that supervision is just another managerial device to keep people on the straight and narrow lines of departmental procedures . . . We seem to be moving towards a red tape model of supervision . . . Maybe this is a logical response to pressure on our profession to become more efficient, effective and economical. But the problem with these developments is that they result in systems which act as if people do not matter. (Veronica Coulshed, 1990[2]).

Another aspect in which grass roots workers feel uncared for and unsupported by managers is in connection with violence. Very few organisations have developed staff care policies and practices around the threat of violence. It is well known that victims of violence often feel personally responsible for what has happened to them and need sensitive counselling to enable them to recover. Managers rarely seem able to oblige. Perhaps this is another example of an inability to stay with pain, or an indication that men are unable to identify with women's legitimate fears of violence.

An anonymous article in *Social Work Today* – 'Workers at risk', (1990) states: 'We need to create a culture that allows the acknowledgement of fear, anxiety and doubt and does not view such expression as threatening or as evidence of weakness . . . which would escape from the macho posturing of "I can handle it" or "it comes with the territory"'. The NALGO report (1989) also found that 'staff were critical of communication with senior managers, and wanted greater recognition of skills. They especially felt the lack of acknowledgement for good work'.

Maggie Lancelot (1990[1]) writes:

> If there is a general sense among staff, especially those operating at the interface, that management is divorced from the fundamental content of their work, and that their managers' priorities are seen as related to management objectives, rather than reflective of the interpersonal nature of service provision, then this . . . will create a devaluation of the process of that service provision. This may serve to affect staff morale, and it may be that instances of 'burnout' are partially caused by working in . . . an environment that does not value the individuals' skills or the emotional fabric of the relationships and tasks that . . . staff are involved in with their clients'.

If supervision and support is lacking at the lower levels of the hierarchy, it usually becomes non-existent at middle or senior management levels. At senior management level, management takes the form of handing out instructions. Senior, and often middle, managers are expected to work independently: 'That's what you are paid for'. To ask for support is often seen as weakness. Most women middle managers miss the supervisory aspect of being managed themselves, particularly as they usually set great store by providing supervision and support for their own staff and are more likely to seek it out for themselves (Ruth Eley, 1986). The Social Services Inspectorate Report into child protection in Staffordshire (Allan Levy,

1991) said 'Team managers expressed strong feelings about being unsupported . . . and the failure of management to recognise the realities of life in the districts'.

Women and promotion

This overemphasis on the control functions of management to the detriment of the care functions means that many women do not wish to identify themselves with management, and therefore do not apply for promotion (Ruth Popplestone, 1979).

Maggie Lancelot (1990[1]) found that 31 per cent of the women social workers she surveyed thought the 'male model' of management was off-putting. The Women and Work Programme (Jane Skinner and Celia Robinson, 1988) found that some of the participants in one of their social services training programmes had decided to opt out of considering entering management for similar reasons. A study of women managers in a Social Services Department (Ruth Popplestone, forthcoming) found that only a third were planning to apply for further promotion. Nearly a quarter did not like what they saw of the next level up: 'the further up the ladder one goes the more one has to play games'; 'I don't have the sort of drive to be an Assistant Director'.

Jalna Hanmer and Daphne Statham (1988) report that a number of women on their 'Social Services Needs of Women' courses 'had made a conscious decision not to seek promotion'. They thought that being a manager meant losing contact with direct practice, with other women, and required the development of characteristics they did not value, such as ruthlessness and making decisions which ignored people's needs. The managers in the Women and Work Programme project (Jane Skinner and Celia Robinson, 1988) were seen as interested in 'pursuing outcomes which were to the benefit of their careers, but which failed either to ensure effective service delivery or to utilise the skills of the female workforce effectively'.

Values and management

It is ironical that the values promoted within the personal social services of caring for the client are so often not translated into values for management. It is understandable that staff who spend their days caring for some of the most damaged and neglected people in society want a more caring and supportive management. Current management theory actually holds that some of the most important tasks of management are to demonstrate concern about the customer (customer care), to value the contribution of staff (staff care), and to make things happen by listening to staff and encouraging initiative and creativity rather than blocking ideas and stifling initiative (Tom Peters, 1987). One of the main themes of Tom Peters and Robert Waterman's (1983) work is that 'excellent' organisations are managed by people who believe in the qualities and potential of people, be they workers or customers. They maintain that this belief must be demonstrated by all managers, by means of policies and the way staff are treated. These views are being heavily promoted in management circles, but have yet to be taken up by the personal social services, despite persistent calls for proper 'staff care' and the image promoted of client care. The importance of the underlying message of current management thinking is that morale and productivity are increased if staff are well cared for has yet to be realised. If these caring functions of management were promoted in the personal social services it is highly likely that more women would be attracted to management posts.

A number of Social Services Departments have, however, got to the stage of producing *value statements*. Here is one example, which incorporates caring values. Interestingly, it was the outcome of an exercise by Kingston Social Services Department in 1988 to examine the communication difficulties of the organisation and to see how things might be improved:

> People should have a right to choice, information, privacy and to be respected as individuals without prejudice. Every person we encounter within the course of our work has the right to be valued and treated with dignity. The Social

Services Department adopts this as a basic value underlining all its work.

The statement is divided into three areas: items which affect the consumer; those which affect staff; and those which affect quality of service. Those concerning staff include:

● providing development and training opportunities;
● involving them at all levels in consultation;
● taking notice of their opinions and feelings irrespective of their position in the organisation;
● ensuring access to effective supervision, consultation and support;
● issuing clear policy and practice guidelines;
● helping to protect them from exploitation and abuse;
● providing the best possible working conditions.

The fact that such a values statement has even been formulated suggests that there is a recognition of the need for consensus throughout a department about the ways in which it will operate; that it is not acceptable for management to work to a different set of values from those in caring roles, and that caring values need to be adopted by the whole organisation.

Social workers and other care staff are paid and sometimes trained for their jobs, but they need help, support and backing to do the job well. It is not easy to provide a respectful and sensitive service to others as a carer if you do not feel respected yourself as a worker. The way staff are managed and how they feel about their employers has a direct effect on the service they themselves give. If staff feel undervalued and alienated they can scarcely be expected to offer a high quality service to their clients.

Women as managers

It is now widely recognised, if not implemented, that in order to provide a service which is appropriate for black people, there must be a physical presence of black and ethnic minority staff at all levels of the organisation. It has not yet been recognised that the same is true of gender (Daphne Statham, 1990). We are so used to men being allowed to provide solutions to women's problems in government, the law, medicine and almost every facet of life, that even in the personal social services we seem content for men to be in charge of the most personal aspects of women's lives, and for men to manage a predominantly female workforce, working mainly with women consumers. If men's prisons were managed by women, if men were expected to discuss their sex problems with women hospital consultants, if all chief police inspectors were women, steps would quickly be taken to redress the balance.

As we saw in Chapter 2, it is no accident that it is women who are in the caring jobs and women who are the clients, because women are held responsible in our society for holding families together, bringing up children, protecting them from abuse, and caring for elderly sick and disabled people. Most of the people in poverty and poor housing are women because they are more likely to be on benefits or in poorly-paid jobs, and most very old people living alone are women, because men die at a younger age. These, then, may be labelled 'women's problems' and it is considered 'women's work' and women's place to deal with them. Curiously, it is not also considered appropriate for women to manage the services provided. As we shall see in later chapters, women often apply for promotion because of a commitment to provide a good service. This implies offering support and backing to those in caring jobs. We are in no doubt that if there were even equal numbers of women and men in management jobs there would be far fewer complaints of the kind we have noted above, and far less of a divide between carers and managers.

Caring and management

In the rest of this chapter we will examine the 'careful use' side of management in more detail.

Recent management theorists have emphasised the need for organisations, if they are to be successful or 'excellent', to put 'customer care' and 'staff care' as a priority. More recently, the concept of 'total quality management' (John Stewart and Kieran Walsh, 1990) has come into prominence. The idea behind this is that each aspect of the organisation is examined to encourage improvement of its quality to the highest possible standard. Women managers have much to offer to these processes because they tend to put aspects of staff care such as supervision and support above administrative concerns in their list of priorities (Ruth Eley, 1986). We also know that women often seek promotion in order to have more influence over improving the service as a whole (see Chapter 5).

Good staff care is not only about putting formal systems and practices in place. It is also about paying careful attention to so-called 'little' things, which are often neglected. For example, remembering that a member of staff needs to leave work on time to collect children, enquiring about the progress of a problem, either work-related or domestic, remembering important anniversaries (for example, of bereavement), actively facilitating those issues which are affecting staff and which need to be pursued at higher levels in the organisation, being liberal in encouragement and praise when a job, however small, has been well done. It is usually women who take the trouble to remember these details, which can make an enormous difference to the way people feel about their work.

These 'caring for' activities require an emotional input for them to be genuine concern and not just a management technique. Unfortunately, men managers often take the view that emotions are out of place at work, even in the personal social services, where emotions form a central part of consumers' interaction with the service.

Even people's basic needs are often neglected by personal social services management. Staff may be crowded into unsuitable and inadequate accommodation, which interferes with their ability to do their jobs. Poor facilities for refreshments and toilets give staff the message that they do not matter. Poor heating and ventilation also affect staff morale. Repairs to buildings, furniture or equipment often take months to complete. Frequently it takes death or serious injury to force management into action over violence to staff.

There are many other 'housekeeping' aspects to management which are often neglected. These require very careful attention to detail, and thought about what ends need tying up and who needs to be told about what decisions. The whole process of preparation for meetings, running them efficiently and 'tidying up' after them is a good example. In order for a meeting to be effective and for decisions to be implemented properly, careful attention needs to be given to time planning so that deadlines will be met smoothly; necessary preparations such as room bookings, giving people sufficient notice of the meeting, planning agendas, collecting information, and getting it out and ready on time, necessary discussions so that members are well prepared; consultation so that everyone concerned will feel properly informed and involved; and information collected and disseminated.

For the meeting itself to run smoothly, members, particularly the person in the chair, must be well prepared and have relevant papers to hand. After the meeting, there is always tidying up to do. The chairperson must ensure that minutes are correct and distributed, and that decisions are implemented, which will probably involve liaising, consulting and informing (verbally or in writing) a range of people. Planning of the next meeting should usually start immediately so that the next cycle runs smoothly.

The reason why so many meetings are demoralising and ineffective is that often these 'housekeeping' tasks have not been done properly because they are regarded as unimportant 'women's work'.

The skills of management

The skills involved in the caring strand of management are above all interpersonal and communication skills, often involving an emotional 'caring for' element. As we know, women are brought up to think about other people's needs, to 'tune in' to others and to listen. This means that they start off at an advantage when it comes to using these skills in management, although they are usually not recognised as useful skills by those on recruitment panels. Women who have done social work training will already have enhanced these skills. Management training can help to transfer skills successfully, and to enhance them in a different context.

The 'housekeeping' tasks of management require additional organising and administrative skills. Women often learn these skills through involvement with domestic activities, particularly bringing up children. They manage a multiplicity of people and activities, all going on at the same time. Modern child care manuals even advocate parents using management skills (*Guardian,* 14 August 1990)

We are not suggesting that the 'housekeeping' aspects of management should be done by women alone. We are seeking to validate some of the skills gained from previous experience and training which women bring to management and other jobs, but which are often either taken for granted or not recognised as relevant. The introduction of National Vocational Qualifications may be a vehicle for changing this situation (see Chapter 6).

Managing work, managing self

Most people do not realise that everyone, whatever their job and whatever kind of life they lead, has management responsibilities and already undertakes management tasks. Everyone has to manage their work, manage themselves and manage their personal life. Here are some examples.

The home help has to manage her workload by planning and organising her visits and fitting all her tasks into an allotted time with each client.

The social worker or probation officer usually has to make her own timetable of visits, phone calls and meetings to cover all the work involved in her case load. She has to assess needs, plan interventions, take decisions, prioritise and evaluate (Veronica Coulshed, 1990[1]).

The care assistant has to assist a certain number of residents with personal tasks, for example dressing or bathing, within a certain length of time.

All these examples call for organising, planning and communication skills if they are to be carried out effectively and sensitively.

'Care management' is a recognition that decisions by practitioners about the level and nature of assistance given to clients are management decisions about time and resources. Everyone has to manage themselves if their lives are to run smoothly; for example, getting up, washing and dressing in order to get to work on time. Those with dependants also have to ensure that children are up and go off to school in time with all the things they need for the school day, or get ready for nursery or a child minder, or that elderly or disabled relatives are dressed and made comfortable.

Successfully running a home and bringing up children requires excellent organisational and planning skills. Such management skills are not usually recognised by those responsible for recruiting to management posts. Our purpose in detailing them is to help us to recognise that the gap between ourselves and 'management' is not as great as we might think. Everyone is a manager in some respects. All care staff have skills which can be transferred to management. The advertisement on the following page makes the point humorously but is also serious, and shows how the work we undertake in the home is so undervalued – not only by men but also by women: 'I don't work; I'm just a housewife'.

Good management requires that both the care and control strands work together. Veronica Coulshed (1990[1]) calls this 'virtuous management' – combining efficiency, effectiveness and economy with 'compassion, integrity and a determination to uphold the humane purposes of social welfare organisations'.

We would like to see women reclaiming management as an activity for which they are well qualified by virtue of some of the skills they acquire through their experience as women – which gives them a headstart in learning how to be managers. We believe that their contribution is sorely needed in organisations which are staffed and used predominantly by women. Management has come to be viewed as an activity associated with 'masculine' values and behaviour. This distorted view accounts for many of the problems between

POSITION VACANT
HOUSEWIFE

Applications are invited for the position of manager of a lively team of four demanding individuals of differing needs and personalities. The successful applicant will be required to perform and co-ordinate the following functions: companion, counsellor, financial manager, buying officer, teacher, nurse, chef, nutritionist, decorator, cleaner, driver, child care supervisor, social secretary and recreation officer.

QUALIFICATIONS
Applicants must have unlimited drive and the strongest sense of responsibility. They must be independent and self-motivated and be able to work in isolation and without supervision. They must be skilled in management of people of all ages. They must be able to work under stress for long periods of time if necessary. They must have flexibility to perform conflicting tasks at one time without tiring. They must have the ability to handle new developments in the life of the team, including emergencies and serious crises. They must be able to communicate on a range of issues with people of all ages, including public servants, school teachers, dentists, doctors, trades people, business people, teenagers and children. They must be healthy, creative, active, and outgoing. They must have imagination, sensitivity, warmth, love and understanding, since they are responsible for the mental and emotional well-being of the team.

HOURS OF WORK
All waking hours and a 24-hour shift when necessary.

PAY
None. Allowances by arrangement with the income-earning member of the team. The successful applicant may be required to hold a second job in addition to the one advertised.

BENEFITS
No guaranteed holidays. No guaranteed sick leave, maternity leave or long-service leave. No guaranteed life or accident insurance. No workers' compensation. No superannuation.

(from *No More Peanuts*, Liberty, National Council for Civil Liberties, 1990) management and staff, and insensitivity towards the needs of both staff and consumers.

In this chapter we have argued that the task of management can be seen as having both care and control strands.

Traditionally the control side has been emphasised, which has been consistent with men being in charge of organisations. There was a brief period in the history of the personal social services when women were recognised to have some relevant skills to offer, but significantly only as children's officers.

Since then the controlling strand has been emphasised, thus encouraging the tendency for men to occupy management posts.

Various studies have found that women tend to have different priorities from men in personal social services management, and we will return to this theme in Chapter 8.

We suggest that the practice of management has been distorted by over-emphasising the control functions. This has had the effect of excluding women and causing a split between the caring functions of the personal social services and its management. We believe that good management requires that the care and control strands work together.

5

Women's Jobs, Women's Careers

So far in this book we have been looking at how caring and support is identified as 'women's work', and how management tends to be identified with men. We noted how women have different ideas from men about what constitutes good management, and do not identify with the way in which it is usually practised. When they become managers, women often have different priorities from men colleagues.

One of the results of this is that women's jobs and careers follow a different pattern from men's. It is often assumed that there is only one type of 'career', which involves moving up a ladder. Although we shall spend some time examining this model, because it is the accepted way of getting into management jobs, it is important to remember that most women either do not get on to the ladders at all, or, if they do, find that there are rungs missing, or that there are not many of them.

Ladders

Most organisations view careers as a series of ladders: some short, some long, some close to each other, some further apart, shaped within a pyramid structure, with one well-paid person directing operations at the top, and many low-paid people at the bottom. Only one ladder goes to the very top of the pyramid, but there are plenty of short ones at the bottom. Some of the short ladders lead to dead ends. Examples of

59

these are specialist activities such as training, or caring for a particular client group.

The ladders are sometimes referred to as 'career paths'. The most well-trodden career path in the personal social services would be in a Social Services Department or Social Work Department and would go something like: social worker → team leader → area manager → assistant director → director. Most ambitious men try to climb the long ladders. Some men manage to jump on to a ladder near the top, others climb up two rungs at a time (Joy Foster, 1990). Following a typical career path assumes that the person on the path works full time all their life, is free to move around to get experience in different kinds of area and job, and can devote long hours to work. Most women are not in a position to fulfil such requirements because of domestic responsibilities or obligations to care for children, men, or elderly or sick dependents. Unlike men, women usually do not have anyone to support them if they have a demanding job. Therefore most women find themselves in jobs which are either not on a ladder at all, for example as cleaners, or in specialist advisory posts; or on short ladders, for example as under-fives workers, occupational therapists, day care and residential workers, and home helps. Home help work would, in theory, provide very relevant experience for someone wanting to be a social worker or a home care organiser. However, most home helps are not in a position to get a professional qualification, let alone adequate in-service training. Home help organisers are often brought in from other organisations, rather than promoting someone with experience of home help work. Neither are home helps likely to be considered seriously for unqualified social work or day care work.

This is an example of 'classism' and sometimes racism, because home help work is undervalued and considered as manual labour, (even though it increasingly involves offering emotional and social support and working as part of multi-disciplinary teams), and is therefore considered to be suitable work for working-class women. However social workers are expected to be 'well educated', that is, middle class, which is a way of safeguarding professionalism and drawing a clear distinction between professional staff and clients.

Home care organisers, although they have a highly responsible and complex management task, are also usually prevented from progressing. Their experience (managing low-status work done by working-class women) is regarded as inadequate for middle and senior management jobs, as is their qualification, if it is not the Diploma in Social Work. Some progress in recognising home helps' skills is being made in Newham Social Services Department (Deborah Cameron, 1990). The home care service has been restructured so that staff work in teams linked to home care organisers, who are in turn linked to the social work teams. This has provided opportunities for home helps to progress to become team leaders. Care management may bring further opportunities to lengthen career ladders for home care staff.

Nursery nursing is another example of a short ladder where skills are grossly undervalued. Nursery work, involved as it is with abused children and parents, is enormously skilled and complex. Nursery managers find it hard to progress unless they have social work qualifications.

Lack of career paths is a way of keeping women and black people 'in their place' in 'women's work'. At the beginning of the twentieth century, when the jobs of secretary and clerk in offices were done by men, they were seen as the bottom rung of the promotion ladder. Many men who started in clerical or administrative jobs ended up as managers, sometimes as chief executives of companies. They did not get stuck at the bottom. In organisations where junior posts are held by men, it is still possible for them to work their way up. Such a career path makes sense because secretaries and administrative staff can learn a lot about the jobs they are servicing through the knowledge they pick up during their day-to-day work. Personal assistants often deputise, unofficially of course, for their bosses. Such staff need management skills for their own jobs such as communication, organisational and planning skills, quite apart from a high level of diplomacy.

However, now that these jobs are regarded as 'women's work', providing support to male bosses, they are usually regarded as a dead end. It is extraordinarily difficult for a secretary to gain promotion except to the position of a more senior secretary. The secretary the boss 'just could not do without' is kept firmly 'in her place'. The introduction of computers is having an interesting effect on administrative work. Some jobs are becoming more boring, but programming and document design offer possible ways forward.

The ladder type of career is based on hierarchical organisations which reward every step up the ladder with more money and more status. This encourages the view that people at the 'top' are superior to those at the 'bottom', and are entitled to give orders, even if they have no personal experience of the work being done. Many of the people at the bottom are expected to service the needs of those higher up. This fits neatly into the hierarchies existing in society, where able bodied white men are at the top, and people are graded according to criteria such as their gender, sexual orientation, race and degree of ability, physical and mental.

This system encourages competitiveness to get to the top because those who are seen to be the most able are most likely to be promoted. Men are more likely to enter into the spirit of this competitiveness than women, who tend to avoid situations they identify as being competitive and aggressive (SSI, 1991). When women do compete, they are often rejected by their peers, both men and women, because competitiveness is not a quality that is admired in women. It is doubtful too whether it is a desirable characteristic to be promoted in the personal social services. The ladder model would place consumers at the bottom, because they have either failed to get on to the first rung, or have fallen off the bottom of society's ladder.

Women who climb a career ladder often do so with different motives from men (Nigel Nicholson and Michael West, 1988). Men are usually keen to obtain more status and pay; women are usually more keen to make an impact by improving the service, or to move up the hierarchy because of their personal interest.

Joy Foster (1988[2]) found that women who reach assistant director level in Social Services Departments are interested in the job rather than its status. They are enthusiastic about their work and their values are about commitment, consolidation, getting on with the task in hand, job satisfaction and fulfilment. Her research indicates that many women are not prepared to sacrifice their commitment to the service in pursuit of higher salaries and status. She found that the major difference between the careers of senior men and women managers was that the women had extensive grounding in professional work, whereas the men had concentrated on a management route. This possibly explains the greater commitment of the women to the quality of the service being offered. Jean Jeffrey, Director of Buckinghamshire Social Services Department, says: 'Women tend to wait to finish off the job and feel ready for promotion. That looking before you leap may appear to slow down your career, but it makes for a solid basis' (Anne Fry, 1991).

Nigel Nicholson and Michael West (1988) identify a difference between climbing ladders within the same organisation and moving between ladders in different organisations. In their study of managers, they found that women are more likely to change organisations to climb ladders than are men. Joy Foster (1988[1]) has identified a different pattern amongst senior managers in the personal social services: 'department hopping' (moving quickly between posts at the same level in order to acquire a bigger salary and higher status) is becoming common amongst men, but it is very rare in women, who seem to have more loyalty to their work and organisations. She found that women senior managers were more likely than men to have worked their way up in one department.

Confidence

Lack of confidence often deters women from attempting to climb career ladders. In a recent study, half of the women interviewed about reasons for not applying for management posts in Bradford Social Services Department (Maggie Lancelot, 1990[1]) gave lack of confidence as a first or second reason.

Another study of women who were already managers in a London Department (Ruth Popplestone, forthcoming) showed that a third of them had needed to be encouraged to apply for promotion by their own managers. They did not have the confidence in their own abilities to do so without being encouraged by someone else. Such encouragement is not always forthcoming, as women are often not considered seriously as 'promotion material' by men managers (Maggie Lancelot, 1990[2]), and hence do not take their own skills seriously. The same group of women managers, all professionally qualified, had felt it necessary to notch up many years' experience in basic grade posts before applying for their first management posts. Only three out of twenty-three had less than five years' experience prior to becoming a manager. The rest had an average of nearly ten years in the field before taking on a management role. Several commented that they felt it necessary to get wide experience in several specialist areas of work before applying for promotion. Joy Foster (1988[2]) has found that women who reach assistant director level in Social Services Departments are likely to have had fifteen years post-qualifying experience. The women directors she studied had at least twenty years' experience before becoming directors.

All this is in sharp contrast to the situation of most men managers in the personal social services, who are not deterred from applying for promotion by their lack of experience. Women looking for jobs usually do not apply if they do not meet all the requirements of the job specification. Ruth Eley (1986) found that the women senior social workers she surveyed did not apply for promotion because they did not see themselves as having the necessary skills and attributes. Men, on the other hand, tend to emphasise the experience they have and are confident about being able to pick up quickly the skills they lack, once they are in the job. They are more likely than women to consider that they have the abilities and skills needed for management posts (Ruth Popplestone, forthcoming).

Women who have not been in paid work for a while usually feel even more lacking in confidence. 'They think their minds are addled, that everything has moved on, that they won't keep up' (Jane Brotchie, 1990). This pervasive lack of confidence often stems from events taking place at the very beginning of women's lives. From the start they are often treated as being less important than if they had been born male. Ann Oakley (1979) found that over half of women expecting their first child in an area of West London wanted a boy, whereas under a quarter wanted a girl. After the birth, nearly half of those who had a girl said they were disappointed.

At school, boys tend to receive more attention from teachers (Carol Nagy Jacklyn, 1991), and are still more likely than girls to be encouraged to take scientific subjects. They also tend to be encouraged more readily into adventurous activities outside the home.

The constant encouragement to women to put others before themselves casts doubt on their self worth. Public images of women do not inspire self-confidence. There are few positive models of successful women at work. Media images of women are either frivolous, relating to their sexual attractiveness, or to their relationships as wives, partners, mothers or daughters, rather than as people in their own right.

A man has only to dress neatly in a suit to be treated seriously for what he is, rather than how he looks. Middle age only serves to make him more important or 'distinguished'. Women appearing in public are judged much more in terms of their physical appearance, according to standards set by men. Style of dress, body shape, hairstyle and make up are all scrutinised and become more exacting at middle age. At all ages women are likely to be patronised and not taken seriously; it is a commonly-held belief amongst women at work that they have to be twice as good as men to succeed.

All this is calculated to undermine confidence in women, thereby enhancing the position of men.

Caring as a 'life's work'

'Ladders' are not the only way of viewing a career, especially for women. We saw in Chapter 2 how caring is part of women's identity, and that their caring work in the home provides a route into paid work, which uses some of the same skills.

Many women working in the personal social services regard caring for others as their 'life's work' (Margaret Ryan and Rennie Fritchie, 1982). They tend to stay many years in one job, and often appear to be unconcerned about increasing their pay or getting promotion. Their job gives them an opportunity to do what is most important for them in life: caring directly for others, sometimes within a special group, for example, children, older people, or people with learning difficulties. Such women sometimes provide examples of extreme devotion to their task, and often derive high job satisfaction.

Localised work

Another group of women organise their paid work to fit around other people they are caring for – children, partners, disabled or elderly relatives, or in-laws. Caring for the family is still considered first and foremost to be the responsibility of women, and 'breadwinning' to be the responsibility of men, despite high male unemployment in recent years. The vast majority of heterosexual women expect to hold responsibility for managing the home, and caring for children and other dependents, and they are often 'grateful' if their partner 'helps' in the home. Some cultures expect young married women to undertake household duties to support a large extended family. Domestic responsibilities affect the working lives of all women to a greater or lesser extent. Those women who either choose or allow caring in the domestic sphere to take first place in their lives usually seek geographically convenient work, with hours to suit. This limits their choice of work and often implies no hope of advancement. Part-time work is almost always badly paid and exploitative. While women in full-time paid employment earn on average 77 per cent of men's pay, part-time women workers earn little over 50 per cent of that of men (Sara Horrell and Jill Rubery, 1991). The majority of these women part-time employees are manual workers. Such patterns suit employers, who have an interest in recruiting a cheap workforce, whose experience as mothers, housewives and daughters substitutes for formal training, and whose availability for low-paid shift work is directly related to their status as dependent women with domestic ties. 'Domiciliary care provides a major source of local employment for women whose children are at school or . . . who have caring responsibilities for adults. It uses the abilities they have developed in domestic situations such as a 'caring attitude' and 'experience in performing the full range of household tasks' (Meg Bond, 1989). People in such jobs are in a 'Catch 22' position: they are often not considered to need any training because they are thought to bring the necessary skills for the job with them, but their skills are not valued sufficiently highly to enable them to move out of low-paid, low-status jobs.

Some single women without family responsibilities also opt for a career pattern which gives priority to personal relationships, particularly when they are younger. We have met many women who do not take their careers seriously because they are hoping to meet 'Mr Right', whose career will then be given priority. Sometimes, when 'Mr Right' does not appear, or turns out to be a disappointment, they give their careers more attention as they get older.

'Interest-led' work

There is another career pattern which some women follow. For many women, interest in the job, doing something they enjoy and are interested in, is more important than status and sometimes more important than salary. For these women, job changes are dictated by their developing interests, personal growth and self-fulfilment, which may even take them down ladders as well as up, but often sideways moves are involved as well. The career of one of the authors has developed in this way. She started off in psychiatric social work, then became interested in adoption and work with elderly people. This latter interest led her to a management post which concerned services for elderly and disabled people. She then moved to a senior management post in a Social Services Department, wishing to influence service delivery, then sideways to another management post in a voluntary organisation. Training was part of both of these management posts, and she followed her developing interest in training into a 'lower level' post involving the management of training. This job led her to become more interested in the skills of direct training, so her next move was again down the hierarchy to a direct training job. Julia Phillipson and Maggie Riley (1990) found that many women take on innovative development posts because these use their creativity and can influence service delivery. Black women often achieve promotion by taking on specialist race posts. Such posts may well be time-limited, and criteria for success are less clear, which may make later career moves more difficult.

Planning careers

Many women believe that domestic responsibilities, whether they have them at present, or may have them in the future, are a reason for not taking their careers seriously. Men tend to plan their careers (Nigel Nicholson and Michael West, 1988), deciding where they want to be and by when. We believe that it is important for everyone, whatever their circumstances, to give some thought to mapping out their career. Women may be very happy for part of their life in a caring or support role, either at home or in paid work or both, but they may not wish to stay there for ever, doing the same job until retirement. We know a woman who got a job as a laundress in a day nursery in her late forties after she had brought up her children. She became very interested in working with the under-fives, and then obtained a job as a nursery assistant in the same nursery. She adored the work and developed her skills with the children. After a few years she became interested in training as a nursery officer. Unfortunately, she could find no one who was willing to sponsor her at that age, and could not afford to pay her own fees. This meant that further promotion was blocked. Had she thought ahead at a younger age, she would have been more likely to be able to fulfil her undoubted potential.

A social worker, nursery officer or day care worker, planning to have children at some stage, may be wise to obtain a more senior post before having children. Otherwise it is likely to be more difficult to progress later on. It is also usually easier to find the time and opportunity to obtain a professional qualification before having children.

It is, of course, not easy to plan ahead. Many women 'wait to see what happens', or have decisions made for them by other people, or organise their lives around other people's. Planning ahead may force us to make uncomfortable choices, such as not always putting other people's needs first. Some women do not plan ahead because they are afraid of being disappointed if plans do not work out. It is a good idea to have 'fall back' arrangements or secondary plans in case the first plan proves unworkable. Plans can be changed if they do not work out, but options may be closed if no plans are made.

Career life planning

Everyone needs regular opportunities to discuss their career and development needs. If opportunities are not available with a manager, it is worth approaching a training officer or other colleague.

Some women seek out a 'mentor': someone in a more senior post who is willing to spend time with them regularly in order to listen, support and counsel about career matters. This has proved to be invaluable to many women in advancing their careers. We also know of a number of mentor schemes which are organised by black people. To be a mentor is something that senior women can do to assist others to advance their careers. Women in more senior positions often do not realise how important they are as role models and examples to other women.

Career life planning workshops can be a helpful way of thinking about work and personal development. There are also organisations whose job it is to advise on careers, usually for a fee, and we include information about some of these at the end of this book. There are some helpful books about career life planning, which we list at the end.

In this chapter we have seen how women's careers tend to follow a different pattern from those of men. Women's domestic responsibilities, lack of opportunity and their motivation to be in an interesting job rather than increase their pay or status are all reasons for this, in addition to lack of confidence and opportunity.

6

Getting into Management

Women who decide to go into management encounter a
number of blocks and barriers in the organisations in which
they work. This is all the more so for black women, disabled
women and lesbians. This chapter will identify some of the
blocks and look at some ways of overcoming them.

We saw in Chapter 2 how people's attitudes about work are
affected by the cultures in which they are brought up and live.
Just as attitudes are affected by the culture of a particular
society, so work experience is affected by the culture of
employment organisations.

The culture of organisations

To understand the meaning of the culture of an organisation it
is helpful to think about what might strike an anthropologist
from another country who had come to study organisations in
which people work. The anthropologist would notice things
about the organisation's habits, values and attitudes such as
policies, how decisions are made and by whom, how people
are treated, how things are organised, the sort of language that
is used, and methods of selection and promotion.

As most employment organisations were set up by white
men and are still controlled by them, it is not surprising that
working arrangements in them are often not suited to
women.

The culture of personal social services organisations has to
some extent been influenced by women because of their

70

presence in large numbers, albeit at the bottom of the hierarchy, often in outposted teams and establishments, which are to some extent independent in the way in which they organise their work. This is one of the reasons women very often find it more comfortable to work in these environments rather than in management groups.

However, many aspects of the culture of the organisations in which we work obstruct women's careers and make them uncomfortable places in which to work. We will look at some examples of this both now and in the next chapter.

Structure

Almost all personal social services organisations are structured like a pyramid. Every job is graded according to how important the work is judged to be, and paid accordingly. Local authorities have systems of job evaluation which determine where jobs should be placed in the hierarchy. The criteria for evaluation reflect values which ensure that caring work remains low-status; for example, responsibility for staff is judged to be more important than responsibility for the same number of clients. The pyramid structure focuses upwards and encourages competitiveness for status and power. Most women dislike the formality and hierarchical nature of these structures, and this is reflected in the structures of women's organisations, which are often modelled in different ways, placing emphasis not on people's status in the organisation, but on respect for the individual and what she can contribute, regardless of her status. Thus women often prefer to structure their organisations as co-operatives, collectives or networks, which minimise differences of status and pay, valuing everyone's contribution and encouraging respect, co-operation and teamwork.

Pyramid organisations are military-style structures which often have many levels in the 'chain of command'. They encourage the process outlined in Chapter 4, of managers getting out of touch with workers. As Mike Pegg (1990) writes, middle managers 'stop the message coming down and the truth going up'.

As all those who have worked in Social Services Departmentments know to their cost, reorganisation of these pyramid structures is a favourite pastime of senior managers. This has been going on for centuries: 'We trained hard, but it seemed that every time we were beginning to form teams we would be reorganised. I was to learn later in life that we tend to meet any new situation by reorganising – and a wonderful method it can be for creating the illusion of progress, while producing confusion, inefficiency and demoralisation' (Roman soldier in AD66, quoted in *Community Care*, 6 July 1989).

Anyone who has been through a major reorganisation knows that it causes years of confusion, anxiety and demoralisation, which bring their toll of human suffering amongst the staff affected. They can also be relied upon to produce a number of better-paid 'jobs for the boys' in management. The end result is another pyramid, which is duly reorganised again a few years later. In some commercial organisations, restructuring is beginning to take place along different lines, more akin to the networks favoured by women's organisations. 'The centre's role is to co-ordinate the activities of many different satellites. It is to protect the organisation's values, clarify the vision, generate vitality and ensure that people deliver visible results. The satellites' role is to play their part in the whole network to reach its common goals'. Julia Ross (1990) considers that such new structures will require leaders with a supportive, rewarding approach who will bring out the best in people, will initiate change and then manage the results of that change'. She considers that women may have an advantage over men in applying these skills 'partly because they have often had to learn those very skills in their child rearing capacity and partly they do not have to unlearn authoritarian behaviour'.

Career paths

Career paths in the personal social services are geared to the working lives of men, demanding full-time work and mobility, with support both at home and at work. Personal social services organisations still regard full-time work throughout the year for thirty-five or forty years as the norm. The only widespread concession to this is 'flexitime', which marginally improves flexibility of working hours. Most women are unable to work full time throughout their working lives and in consequence suffer in terms of low pay and lost promotion, or sacrificing domestic life to fit into the male world of work. Although there are many part-time jobs in the personal social services most of them are low-paid and at the bottom of the hierarchy. They are often not seen as 'proper' jobs and have very poor conditions of service. There are very few part-time management jobs. In 1989, 22 per cent of field social work posts were part-time, but only 3 per cent of team leaders (SSI, 1991). Women who are promoted before a career break often return to a basic grade job because there are no senior posts available, or because management jobs are not part-time. A survey in Coventry Social Services Department in 1979 (Veronica Beechey and Tessa Perkins, 1987) found that 63 per cent of the workforce worked part time, most of them were women, and most were not considered to need professional training. Most part-timers are also white (SSI, 1991). Maternity leave is a relatively recent innovation and not sufficiently flexible for many women. It has not significantly affected the numbers of women who work continuously (SSI, 1989). A survey of three Social Work Departments (SSI, 1991) showed that one third of the women employed had taken a career break, but only 9 per cent had returned after maternity leave. Carers' or dependants' leave, which recognises caring responsibilities for elderly relatives and includes leave for lesbians and gay men, is even less common. Job sharing schemes, where they exist, offer opportunities for promotion to those who cannot work full time. However, management posts are not always included. Career break schemes, which have been developed in a number of commercial organisations, are virtually non existent. Workplace nurseries are few and far between.

Only when demographic trends threatened to produce serious staff shortages did employers begin to make an effort to be more flexible in order to attract and retain more women. To our knowledge, this has not yet reached the ears of the personal social services, even though it has an estimated national shortage of 2200 social workers and 250 occupational therapists (Jane Brotchie, 1990), but the civil service has begun to make the sort of far-reaching changes in conditions of employment for everyone that could really benefit women.

For example, a *Guardian* report (27 July 1990) says that the Treasury now offers the same promotion and training opportunities and pensions benefits to part-timers as to full-timers. 'Part time' has come to have a wider meaning: for example, people can choose to work school terms only. Employees can take special leave for child care or to care for elderly relatives, for voluntary work or for other experience. Staff on special leave can apply to be reinstated on the same grade and at the same point in the salary scale as when they left. A formal career break scheme for child or elderly relative care keeps them in touch with the work of the office and encourages them back from time to time to catch up on latest developments. They can come back part time if necessary. A number of departments are operating home-working schemes on computers provided by the department. Such schemes must become much more widely available if women are not to be penalised in their career development.

Values

The values of the organisation are reflected in numerous ways, such as the posters on the walls, the photographs on people's desks (which often depict images which objectify or exclude women, black people, disabled people or lesbians), or the qualities required of managers. We noted in Chapter 2 how frequently advertisements for non-management staff contain references to 'caring'. There is a remarkable absence of such words in advertisements for management posts. They are more likely to contain words like 'objectivity', 'targets', 'analytical', 'tough', 'control', 'decisiveness', 'achievement', 'determination', 'goals', or 'monitoring', and emphasise the rewards of high status, salary and related 'packages', (which usually include a fast car) to attract applicants, obviously designed to reflect the status of the post. Such advertisements, consciously or unconsciously, are designed to attract white, able bodied men, and modelled on the values of the boys' public school system. It is interesting to speculate about what an advertisement designed to attract women would contain. Undoubtedly the list of qualities and skills required would be different. The 'package' would be more likely to offer longer holidays, continuing training and child care arrangements than fast cars.

Sexual harassment

The phrase 'sexual harassment' was unknown only a few years ago. This meant that many women were unable to put a meaning to this version of the abuse of power by men: the systematic, repeated and unwanted advances, physical and verbal, which threaten and humiliate, undermine job performance, perhaps block promotion or training opportunities, and are perpetrated even by 'right on' men. Women still sometimes blame themselves for these incidents, believing that they might have handled the relationship better. Sometimes sexual harassment leads to resignation of the woman because it becomes too uncomfortable for her to continue working with the culprit. Now at least there is language to describe such behaviour. Working women are becoming more outspoken, and widespread sexual aggression at work is being uncovered and challenged (Michael Rubenstein, 1988). Increasingly, employers are devising policies for dealing with sexual harassment.

However, it is a courageous woman who initiates a formal complaint and sees it through. Most women do not have access to legal advice, or adequate support, and many feel too humiliated and powerless to take action. To deal with these problems a group of women in Leeds Social Services Department (SSI, 1991) have been trained to support women through the process. There are also support organisations such as Women against Sexual Harassment, and Women's Legal Defence Fund.

Trade unions

Unfortunately, trade unions are not well known for their activities in relation to women's issues. They are rather like traditional men's clubs, dominated by white men whose style and language is often intimidating to women, who may not understand the protocol and dislike aggressive bargaining tactics. This despite the fact that NALGO (National Association of Local Government Officers) had a 53 per cent female membership and NUPE (National Union of Public Employees) 75 per cent in 1989 (*Equal Opportunities Review*, 1990).

Several studies carried out in the 1970s and 1980s came to the conclusion that men ran the unions and women felt that that the unions did not belong to them. Cynthia Cockburn (1987) wrote: 'Women workers are still not seen as the norm, even by many trade union men. The typical member of the workforce is seen as a male, white, fulltime, life-time worker . . . the same hierarchy of power that exists in employment is allowed to exist within many unions. Because women are not "important" employees, they are not seen as important union members'. Only 8 per cent of NUPE's full time officials are women, and 3 per cent of NALGO's. Although these unions have equal opportunities policies, negotiations on behalf of huge numbers of women workers are still carried out by men.

According to a report published in 1984 (C. Brown, 1984), black and Asian women were more inclined to join unions and participate in union activities than were white women, but less likely to hold positions of power. A TUC (Trades Union Congress) report in 1987 stated 'Racism not only prevents black and ethnic women and men gaining employment in the first place, it also militates against union activity to improve their position in employment and within the union. Additionally, often, racism and sexism go hand in hand'.

Women are often claimed to 'lack confidence' in taking part in union activities. Cynthia Cockburn (1987) comments 'What lies behind the confidence factor is intimidation by the masculinity – both in terms of sheer presence and of style – of union committees, branches, conferences. The role model for unionism is male'. Anna Coote and Polly Pattullo (1990) found that 'There was a tendency to overlook the way in which employment was inextricably bound up with the rest of life – reflecting men's narrow preoccupation with paid as opposed to unpaid work. Unions consequently saw the worker in limited terms and failed to cater for the "whole human being". They used coded jargon and procedures, their style of operation often seemed very 'masculine' – aggressive and confrontational rather than seeking consensus. Not all unions were guilty of all these faults, but all these observations were made regularly by women exploring the reasons for their relatively low level of participation.'

They quote Ivy Cameron, a union national negotiator: 'There's a silly emphasis on a macho way of negotiating. It's bad for the health of the individuals concerned and it doesn't tackle the really important issues like low pay. A lot of time is wasted in rituals: the big build up to the annual pay round and months spent haggling over half a per cent. Would it not be better to go in and talk about job evaluation, flat rate increases, restructuring, equal value? And what's the point of shouting across the table . . .? There are other ways of bargaining – more co-operative and less confrontational – which take less time, create less hostility and tension, and get better results'.

Some unions have made an effort to draw upon women's values to create a new culture. In 1975 NUPE introduced five reserved seats on its national executive for women. By 1986 women held a total of eleven seats. In 1982 they set up a network of women's advisory committees, appointed a women's officer and started a programme of training for women. Between 1974 and 1984 the proportion of women shop stewards increased from 28 per cent to 42 per cent. Women particularly valued the opportunity to meet without men. Anna Coote and Beatrix Campbell (1987) quote women members of NUPE: 'If more women could get together in small groups . . . that would build up confidence. We couldn't have spoken freely if men had been there'. Another discovered for the first time that other women shared her ideas and feelings: 'I used to think it was just me'. Some unions employ counsellors to support and advise victims of sexual harassment.

Although there are large numbers of women members in the unions covering personal social services organisations, as yet most of them receive a very poor service from their unions, which are still largely concerned with obtaining percentage pay increases for their members. Since most women are amongst the low-paid, a percentage rise is of less value to them than to the majority of men. Equal-pay claims, which are potentially of much greater value, are rarely pursued.

In 1990 the TUC announced its intention to draw up a negotiators' equal rights charter (*Equal Opportunities Review*, 1990). This should encourage negotiators to concentrate on particular issues which will include claims for equal pay, equal opportunities recruitment procedures, child care facilities and improvements in maternity pay.

Equal opportunities policies

Equal opportunities policies are an attempt to ensure that all employees or potential employees of an organisation have equal rights and opportunities. They attempt to eliminate discriminatory practices such as those we have already mentioned and to take positive action to make up for past disadvantage. Local authorities have pioneered this approach, which has had mixed success.

Some organisations merely confine themselves to a statement indicating that they are an 'equal opportunities employer'. Others have clearly worked out policies and training strategies. Veronica Coulshed (1990[1]) writes: 'Unfortunately it is too easy for employers to boast that they have an equal opportunities policy . . . in reality there may be no accompanying resources, policy changes or changes in practice'. She reports how in Liverpool prior to 1980 'even though there was high unemployment amongst the black community . . . the local authority had not felt it necessary to have an equal opportunities policy'.

Those organisations which are serious about equal opportunities have reorganised the job recruitment process in order to combat discriminatory practices at each stage. Usually each aspect of the process is examined and changes made to try to provide equal opportunities for all groups. The wording of advertisements is carefully scrutinised to ensure that the language used is not off-putting or so worded that it is likely to attract only one sector of the population. Care will be taken to ensure that advertisements are placed in papers and journals which will be seen by members of groups that are under-represented in the workforce; for example magazines read by women, such as *Everywoman* or *Spare Rib*, or by black people, such as *The Voice*.

In order to eliminate bias in the selection procedure, application forms are modified so as not to ask for information which is irrelevant or discriminatory. First attempts have eliminated reference to marital status, number of children and in some cases first names, but date of birth is still requested. Criteria are agreed for the necessary qualifications and skills for each post, but of course these are influenced heavily by the conception of the job held by those already in post.

Questions are then prepared which relate directly to the criteria in order to reduce the scope for personal questions at whim which have nothing to do with the person's skills and are often in breach of the sex discrimination and race relations laws. All women have horror stories about questions they have been asked at interview about their personal lives which would never be asked of men. Disabled people are similarly often patronised because of their disability or not taken as seriously as an able bodied person with the same qualifications. Interviewing which incorporates equal opportunities principles aims to enable candidates to be judged more fairly on whether they possess the necessary skills for a post, rather than relying on the panel's 'intuition', which is often founded on prejudice. The composition of the panel may also be scrutinised. Many women and black people feel at a disadvantage if they are interviewed by a group of white men.

Yet however much the content of interviews and the conduct of panels is manipulated, the process of being interviewed formally is still inherently discriminatory. Most men thrive on being given the opportunity to talk about themselves and their achievements. For most women it is an alien and intimidating experience. 'Blowing your own trumpet' or boasting about achievements is not something women thrive on. People chosen by individual interview are more likely to be those who fit in with the management culture than those who are acceptable as managers to the groups they have to work with most of the time. Equal opportunities policies mean that these people no longer have any say in the appointment process and there is no testing of the candidates' performance in a group except at very senior levels.

Whilst some organisations have been more concerned about promoting a positive image than creating real change and making a difference to the experience of their employees, such measures do seem to have gone some way towards achieving a more mixed workforce in some places.

Birmingham Social Services Department achieved a 10 per cent increase between 1984 and 1987 in the number of women managers. Lambeth achieved a considerable increase in the number of disabled people on the staff of the council after a determined campaign (*Equal Opportunities Review*, 1990). The same was true in Birmingham where disabled people's needs in the workplace are taken seriously (*Equal Opportunities Review*, January/February 1990).

Equal opportunities employers have introduced a variety of other measures to limit discrimination, such as workplace nurseries, job sharing schemes, and policies on sexual and racial harassment. A survey by the Institute of Manpower Studies (Hilary Metcalf, 1990) asserts that local authorities offer the most generous working conditions and employment policies to attract and retain women employees.

Workplace nurseries have been a very popular measure and effective in enabling more women to return from maternity leave and apply for promotion. However, demand for work-based child care greatly outstrips supply. Only thirty-four local authorities have workplace nurseries. Compared with other European countries, British employment and child care policies are badly outdated and Britain is falling further behind in its provision of child care and maternity rights (European Commission, 1991). Virtually every other country in Europe has accepted that there is a public responsibility for providing child care (*Equal Opportunities Review*, September/October 1990). The United Kingdom has the shortest period of paid maternity leave and some of the strictest criteria for eligibility, which exclude two out of three part-time workers. It is one of the three member states which has no provision for parental leave, paid or unpaid, and it has the second worst record for child care provision for 3 to 5-year-olds. Only Portugal has less provision for this age group, and France, Italy and West Germany have double the amount of provision in Britain.

Job sharing schemes which enable people at all levels in the organisation to work part time in reasonably well paid jobs have enabled some white women to move into management who would not otherwise have had the opportunity. However, little attention has been paid to the promotion and effective implementation of job sharing, even though there is evidence that it can have a strong influence on the proportion of white women returning from maternity leave (*Women and Training*, 1991).

Policies on sexual and racial harassment give more legitimacy to women and black people asserting their rights in the workplace, but disciplinary procedures are often not effective. Recent initiatives taken by Manchester City Council and Gloucestershire County Council involve targets for the employment of women, ethnic minorities and disabled people. For instance, Manchester has set a target of 33 per cent of Principal Officers and above to be women by 1994, with 3.5 per cent of these posts to be occupied by black women by 1997. Birmingham Social Services Department's target is that half of its managers should be women. In Gloucestershire achievement of the targets is in some cases part of the assessment for performance-related pay of managers.

The director of personnel for the National Health Service suggested that there should be a requirement on managers to establish a given percentage of women at each management level within three years: 'I would attach sanctions through their annual performance review scheme' (Eric Caines, 1991).

Employing women in senior management posts and council positions can make a big difference to the culture of organisations. The London Borough of Southwark was one of the few councils to have simultaneously a woman chief executive, Anna Wyatt, and a woman leader, Anne Matthews.

Anna Coote and Polly Pattullo (1990) report that 'women in the borough found that this made a considerable change in their relationship with the council'. They quote two workers at the Rotherhithe Community group as saying: 'Going to see the council leader used to be like going to see JR in Dallas. But it's not like that any more. The atmosphere has completely changed. There isn't a big drinks cabinet – Anne just makes you a cup of coffee. And she's so accessible. You can phone her up about anything'. Anna Wyatt commented: 'It continually shocks me how male working cultures are not about delivery. They're about status, position, about *being* not *doing*. Women want to see results, are prepared to be flexible, and make changes in themselves'.

Margaret Hodge, leader of the council in Islington, also recognised the change in atmosphere as more women gained political power: 'Women are gentler. All those radical men from 1982 onwards are such bloody chauvinists. They out-shout you. They bully you . . . We've just changed from having a woman as chair of the Labour group to a man, and you can really sense the difference – there's much more shouting across the room' (Anna Coote and Polly Pattullo, 1990). We shall return to the topic of management style in Chapter 8.

Equal opportunities initiatives taken so far have only scratched the surface of discrimination. Taking equal opportunities seriously is a very costly business. However, as Anna Coote and Polly Pattullo (1990) point out, an increasing number of local authorities and voluntary organisations are adopting equal opportunities policies, and these are now spreading to the private sector.

The successful media campaign which was waged against the 'loony left' had the effect of slowing the pace of the development of policies, particularly in connection with lesbians and gay men. There have been casualties due to poll tax capping and there is a danger of equal opportunities being undermined by contracting out. 'The Treasury has conceded that "most of the savings from contracting out arise because contractors offer poorer conditions of employment"' (HM Treasury, 1986; quoted by Tim Booth, 1990).

Applying for jobs

Some women feel that applying for jobs in organisations which have refined their procedures is now so complicated and intimidating that they sometimes decide it is not worth trying. Unfortunately, it is not usually realised that help can be obtained from the personnel department. Some local authorities enclose guidance for completing application forms with all information sent out about jobs.

The most important thing to remember when applying for jobs in organisations with an active equal opportunities policy is that candidates must provide evidence, both on the application form and at interview, that they can fulfil the selection criteria or person specification. This is also valuable advice in applying for any job.

Women who want to become managers may be more likely to be successful in organisations where there is an active equal opportunities policy, but some of these organisations are unfortunately more concerned with their image than in changing their practices.

Women in organisations where there is no policy or where the statement is not backed up by detailed policies may wish to take action to draw discrimination to the attention of the policy makers. In some organisations women have researched the position of women in the organisation either formally, perhaps as a project or piece of research for an academic course, or informally as a group. It is often relatively easy to obtain figures from the personnel section giving the number of women and men at different levels of the organisation. Producing this information to the right people – councillors or senior managers – at an opportune time, can serve to draw attention to discrimination against women.

Family values and women staff

Because of the nature of the work of the personal social services which often involves breakdowns in relationships between people, particular prominence is given to values about family life and women's role within it. Blame for breakdown in family relationships is often attached to women not making themselves available to act as the centre and support, physical and emotional, to other family members. Such values can put severe strains on women staff, particularly those with young children, who may feel reproached by colleagues for being working mothers and paying someone else to look after their child. It is perfectly common and acceptable for men managers to have a young family and to experience little or no conflict, because there is a woman at home looking after the children. The strains of finding and keeping good quality child care typically fall on mothers. Many women feel guilty when care arrangements break down, and fear that they are not pulling their weight at work as well as not providing proper care for their child.

There are no easy answers to this situation, but it is important to recognise that it is not just an individual problem. It arises because of the way in which society operates in the Western world: families exist very separately in small groups with very little mutual support; responsibility for the physical and emotional care of children is vested largely in the mother and she is blamed when things go wrong; there is a great stress on individual responsibility and on 'ownership' of children by parents. In societies where extended families are the norm there is far more mutual aid and a series of adults on whom children can depend. Going to work is not a problem if children can easily be left with another member of the household or taken to work. As we have seen, Britain is out of step with many other Western European countries, where day care for young children is much more readily available. Over the last half century in Britain the availability of day care has fluctuated according to the needs of the country for women to be part of the workforce. During the war women were actively encouraged to go back to work to assist the war effort. Day nurseries were set up to enable this to happen. But as soon as the servicemen came back from the war propaganda was put out about the desirability of women being at home to care for the family in order to release jobs for the men (Ronald Walton, 1975). This was backed up by the writings of child psychologists, for example, John Bowlby

(1967), and the closure of nurseries. These views were reinforced in the 1960s by widespread pejorative remarks about 'latch-key' children, implying that they were being neglected because their mothers were not at home to give them tea on their return from school. In other circumstances this concern could have been translated into widespread after-school care schemes, or more flexibility in employment arrangements for both women and men. In the late 1980s, concern started to grow about labour shortages on account of the diminishing number of school leavers, which resulted in some employers beginning to take responsibility for day care for children to enable more women to return to or stay at work. However, workplace nurseries are not the answer to all child care problems, and a much wider discussion needs to take place about the responsibilities of men, women and the state for providing high-quality child care.

Caring, the family and work

Women are not only expected to be the primary physical carers in the home, but also the main source of emotional care and support to partners and children. What is often not recognised is that heterosexual women cannot expect anything remotely comparable in return for the amount of caring and support they give to others. This puts them at an enormous disadvantage compared with male colleagues because they have to provide their own support (Ruth Popplestone, forthcoming). Many women consider themselves lucky if their partners even tolerate them going out to work. There is a different dynamic for Afro-Caribbean women, who have never been able to take the family for granted. They have always had to fight to hold on to family life. Black women often find support for themselves and their culture in the family in a racist society.

It is significant that the vast majority of men managers in the personal social services are married, often with young children. Marriage for men implies a high degree of emotional support from a woman, and lends a degree of respectability to the man. Research shows that most women managers are single or divorced, and very few have young children (Ruth Popplestone, forthcoming). Joy Foster's study of Assistant Directors (1988[2]) found that three-quarters were single or divorced and only 18 per cent had responsibility for children. The majority of the men were married and had children.

Unless she is in a lesbian partnership, the typical woman manager is unlikely to have the built-in emotional support at home which is taken for granted by her male counterparts. Even if she is married, her husband is very unlikely to provide much practical or emotional support (Ruth Popplestone, forthcoming). Research shows that men managers have wives, and that if women managers have partners, they are working partners. 'For men marriage provides a platform of support and security from which to launch their careers, while for women it is a competing demand and an obstacle (Sandra Langrish, 1981). Half the men in one study of managers had full-time housewives as partners, while less than one in ten of the women had a non-employed partner. Barely a quarter of the men had full-time working partners, but 90 per cent of the women faced the problem of co-ordinating their career demands with their partner's full-time work obligations (Nigel Nicholson and Michael West, 1988). This study also showed that almost half the women managers were childless, but only one in ten of the men were. Even then the women had smaller families than the men: 'There is a strong suggestion here that married women are either forgoing or at least postponing the role of mother for the sake of their careers, and when they do have families they are limiting their family size to minimise competing role obligations' (Nigel Nicholson and Michael West, 1988).

We also know that women put a higher value on support from others at work (Ruth Eley, 1986), either formally through supervision or informally through colleagues. This may well be a reflection of the fact that they cannot rely on opportunities to discuss their work problems at home. This is also why supportive friendships at work and in personal life are so important to women.

'Networking' (the process of seeking and providing supportive contacts for work purposes) has become an important means by which women can make up for the lack of support that is often forthcoming from bosses, and also from home. Because of their awareness of their own need for support at work, women are sensitised to the needs of others, and often place a high value on providing support at work for others. There is a another side of this coin, however. Those women who are resentful about the amount of caring that is expected of them in all contexts may be unwilling to offer it and once again fall into the 'caring trap'.

Career development

Many social workers are very critical of the supervision they receive. Even when supervision is available, the emphasis is usually on accountability and rarely provides scope for discussion about career advancement (Margaret Richards, Chris Payne and Annie Sheppard, 1990). Some organisations have a system of appraisal, which may provide such opportunities, but not always where women are concerned.

A study of the probation service (Owen Wells, 1983) found that women probation officers believed that they stood less of a chance of achieving promotion than did men. This was not actually borne out in practice, but it was found that in their appraisal sessions the question of career development was less likely to be raised in interviews with women probation officers than with their male colleagues. Jane Skinner and Celia Robinson (1988) point out that where there is not a systematic appraisal system, people's career potential will probably be judged according to their similarity to existing (men) managers.

One of the reasons why there are more men in management posts is simply that men make more applications. A study of men and women teachers found that some men made dozens of applications before getting promotion (S. Hilsum and K. Start, 1974). One moral of this for women is to keep on applying if they want to be promoted, and not to give up if the first few applications are not successful. Many women see failure to get a particular job as a personal slight and are easily put off making other applications. They often wait until there is a job advertised which they really want before making an application, but it is necessary to get practice in applying for jobs and going for interviews. Like anything else, it is a skill which has to be learned. Some employers offer unsuccessful applicants an opportunity to get feedback on the reasons for their rejection. This is an valuable way of finding out about anything which might be improved next time round, as long as the person giving the feedback does it in a professional manner.

Because women, and particularly black women, are usually not seen as obvious candidates for management they are often overlooked when there is an opportunity for taking an acting-up position. They are also more likely to act-up for longer periods of time and then not necessarily get the job (Joy Foster, 1990). However, an acting position is a valuable opportunity to get experience in a more senior job and to prove ability to do the job. Women need to make themselves visible so that when opportunities arise they are not passed over. Some women believe that if they keep their heads down and do a good job they will be noticed. Unfortunately, this is not usually the case. Any woman who is interested in promotion must let other people know and ensure that her work is noticed. It is also sometimes necessary to create opportunities to provide the experience needed for a more senior job. Women need to look out for opportunities to take on tasks and projects which will enhance their experience. Taking initiatives and offering to take on responsibility when there are tasks which need doing can provide useful additional experience. It is a mistake to assume that it is not possible to continue getting useful experience on maternity leave. Indeed, it is important to keep in touch so that this period is not just a blank on the *curriculum vitae*.

It is always possible to obtain valuable experience in local community groups in such activities as committee work, fund raising and local politics. Some employers are beginning to realise that a career break can provide a very positive stage in career development. Recent research shows that informal learning contributes very significantly to career development (Cathy Hull, 1990).

There are several good books on the market that can help to develop skills. Working through a book such as *A Manager's*

Guide to Self Development (Mike Pedler, John Burgoyne and Tom Boydell, 1986) would be a very good preparation for anyone wishing to move into management.

Many women get stuck because of not having a professional qualification or suitable in-service training. Gaining professional qualifications is a real problem now that it is so much more difficult to obtain funding for full-time training. The Central Council for the Education and Training in Social Work produces a helpful leaflet on funding (CCETSW, 1992) which is worth consulting. Women also miss out on post-qualifying training. In 1988 the proportion of men taking post-qualification courses was 43 per cent, compared to 29 per cent on qualifying courses (SSI, 1991).

Training

At the end of the 1980s the National Council for Vocational Qualifications (NCVQ) was set up to provide a system of qualifications at different levels across all employment sectors. National Vocational Qualifications (NVQs) should help women in at least two ways. Firstly, the level at which they are working will be assessed and recognised. This will be an important means for recognising skills gained through previous experience and training which currently go unrecognised, both in the many so called 'unskilled' jobs which are regarded as 'women's work', and in management tasks. Competence-based qualifications define work as 'purposeful activity with critical outcomes'. Whether it is paid work or domestic, community or volunteer work is irrelevant to the fact that people can acquire competence while doing it. Competence is defined as the ability to perform in paid work to the standard required. What matters is that the person can do the job, not how they acquired their competence. Unpaid work can therefore count towards qualifications. The NCVQ and the Royal Society of Arts (RSA) have already decided to recognise competence acquired through unpaid work, and other bodies awarding qualifications are likely to follow their lead. The Employment Department Training and Employment Directorate is to fund a study of unpaid work in the home which will analyse competences acquired in running a home (Linda Butler, 1991). The second way in which NVQs may help women is that they are likely to bring more opportunities for in-service training that will lead to nationally recognised qualifications at a number of levels, thus offering the opportunity for progression. It remains to be seen whether it will be possible to progress through to the Diploma in Social Work by this route. Information about training can be obtained from the training section of employing organisations or from the NCVQ or CCETSW. Addresses of these organisations are given in the Appendix at the end of this book.

Women wishing to advance their careers should obtain as much training as possible. Find out what opportunities are available for in-service training or short courses in your own organisation. If it is not possible to obtain training through work, consider undertaking a distance learning course such as the Open College's 'Moving into Management', the Open University's 'Women into Management' or courses based on the 'Springboard Workbook'. Addresses where you can find out about these courses are given at the end of this book. It is sometimes possible to get an employing organisation to pay either in whole or in part for such courses. Information is available through the training section.

Women who have no qualifications, or feel they need help in basic study skills, might consider a 'Return to Study' course. These are designed for people who missed out in their education and help to increase confidence and improve basic reading and writing skills. Such courses may be based at a local college or adult education institute. Local libraries can provide information about courses in your area.

In this chapter we have looked at a number of blocks and barriers encountered by women who wish to progress in management. We have examined how equal opportunities policies have set out to counter discrimination, and assessed their effectiveness towards this end.

7

Being in Management

In previous chapters we have talked about the problems women face in getting into management posts. This chapter will concentrate on what it is like to be a woman manager.

A few personal social services organisations, usually in the big cities, already have fairly large numbers of women in middle management, and equal opportunities policies are in some places influencing the number of women in senior management posts. At the time of writing, in one Social Services Department half the senior managers were women. This is probably partly due to the fact that there was both a woman chair of the Social Services Committee and a woman director. However, many women managers have to face isolation at work because they are cut off from other women and are often the only woman in their working group. Meg Bond (1989) writes: 'In moving into residential management I moved to a tier beyond which few women and even fewer black colleagues had progressed. All my immediate peers were white men. Above me it was a white man's world.'

It is often difficult to remain part of support networks when promoted to senior management. On the one hand, the newly promoted woman may be the object of suspicion and jealousy from former peers. On the other, she may fear being disloyal to her new peer group if she is to be honest with the previous one. One of the authors was criticised by her director for remaining in close contact with social workers when she was a senior manager.

What women bring to management

Although we will be talking in the next chapter about some of the common factors that women believe they bring to management, it is, of course, important to bear in mind that there is an enormous diversity in what they bring. We want to value the rich variety of contributions that women of different races, classes, religions and outlooks contribute. It is frustrating to women and a loss to society that so much talent is unused because organisations have such limited views as to what constitutes 'suitable management material'.

We have noticed, both in our experience and through research (Joy Foster, 1988[2]) that women managers usually bring enormous enthusiasm and commitment to their work. Sometimes their enthusiasm becomes diluted after many years in the job, but their commitment to doing the job well seems to remain.

The reasons for this are probably that women managers are breaking new ground. They do not come into management as a matter of course as many men do. (Ruth Popplestone, forthcoming). As many women managers point out, women have to be twice as good as men in order to get the job. A black woman assistant director wrote: 'You can't be mediocre or awful like some white managers are. You . . . have to be far better' (Josie Durrant, 1989).

Two of the writers have run a number of courses for women managers. One feature of many of these courses is the dramatic change that takes place as the women present recognise and begin to value their contribution to management. Women are so influenced by the lack of validation, recognition and encouragement (Ruth Eley, 1989) that they get on a day-to-day basis in organisations operating on an entirely different value system fashioned by men, that they can easily lose sight of their own skills and qualities as women. Reclaiming our own values and recognising our own power in the company of other women can be a liberating experience.

What happens to women managers

So what happens to women managers that causes them to lose

sight of their values and skills? As an example, we will look at the processes at work when one woman is appointed to a male-dominated management group (see video produced by Ora Fant *et al.*, 1980).

When someone who is noticeably different joins an existing group, say a woman or a black person joining a group of white men/people, their differences cause a threat to the values and habits of the group. The usual response is strong pressure from the group to neutralise the difference so that it does not have to be taken seriously and can therefore cause the group members to question their attitudes and behaviour. A common technique to achieve this is to absorb the newcomer, thus rendering her ineffective in bringing about change: 'We would love to have you but you will have to conform'. She then becomes 'one of the boys', and takes on a lot of their understanding about 'the way things are' and starts behaving like them, sometimes even to the extent of the way she dresses (dark suit, bow tie, and so on). Martin Willis (1990) quotes a woman manager who spoke of the pressure to participate in male sexual banter because to challenge it runs the risk of not being accepted. However much she allows herself to be absorbed, the woman manager is excluded from the informal and social contact between men in the pub or the toilet, which helps to 'oil the wheels' (Ruth Eley, 1986).

Another technique to render someone ineffective is to isolate her by emphasising the differences, and ridiculing her or ruling her out of court, questioning her competence or giving her lower status than the rest of the group. Black women managers are often identified as race specialists, which is usually interpreted as being a narrower role than mainstream management jobs. They are expected to bring about change, but also to 'fit in' and not challenge existing assumptions or ways of working (SSI, 1991).

For this technique to work the woman must either keep quietly on the sidelines, perhaps fitting into a servicing role, where she can be dismissed as 'ineffectual', or fight back and be labelled as 'aggressive', 'unfeminine', 'hysterical' or 'bossy'. She may also be considered 'humourless' when she fails to laugh at sexist comments or jokes. Senior black women have described feeling by-passed and marginalised in organisations where power remains firmly in the hands of white groups (SSI, 1989).

The competence of black managers can become 'the subject of discussion and open scrutiny, reinforcing the myth of black people not being up to the job. In direct contrast, white managers are allowed to make mistakes and are often helped to identify programmes to rectify the gaps in their knowledge' (Waveney Williams, 1991).

In order to avoid these traps, the newcomer must be willing to be a pioneer. She must gain sufficient acceptance by the group not to be dismissed or marginalised, but also assertively challenge behaviour she finds unacceptable.

Lone women managers can feel very isolated and vulnerable, without support or role models. They are also very visible and experience pressure to prove that women can do the job, feeling that if they fail they will jeopardise the position of other women. They may want to perform all the tasks undertaken by their male colleagues to an exemplary standard, and also offer support and encouragement to large groups of staff (SSI, 1989).

It is not surprising that the lone woman in a male-dominated management team often gives in and succumbs to her role expectations or gives up and retreats to work with other women. We are surprised that we do not hear about more 'aggressive' women managers, for they have a right to be very angry at the way they are squeezed out.

It is no answer to expect one woman to change the culture of a management group, just as it is unfair to expect one black person to bring about changes in attitudes about race.

In order to avoid the trap of being a 'token woman', it is necessary to have both a clearly worked out strategy and massive support from other women. It is very much better if two women can be promoted at the same time to give each other support. It is also important to realise that if all women chip away at sexist attitudes wherever they are it all mounts up. For all we know, the man we are challenging at work may be getting the same treatment at home from his partner. It is encouraging that a few men have changed as a result of being influenced by women, and that there are now men who are prepared to work with women to bring about change.

Organisational culture

There are numerous obstacles and discomforts facing women in the workplace on a day-to-day as well as a long-term basis. This is because organisations behave as though they were still staffed only by men. Men managers usually behave either as though they are fighting a battle or playing a competitive game. In either case they are 'playing to win'. This culture permeates the organisation. There is often a competitive atmosphere, usually played out most conspicuously in the relationship between management and unions (described as 'thug culture' by one woman assistant director), and in the race to line yourself up for the next promotion. Competition is sometimes stimulating and constructive, but more often it diverts people from the main purpose of their work into petty rivalries or doing other people down. This process often involves currying favour with influential people, behaving in ways which reflect glory on himself rather than taking the best course of action for the service, playing power games, 'stabbing in the back', and being seen in the right places by the right people. This can mean drinking in certain pubs, or staying behind to 'work' after hours.

The notion of the war or game also emerges in the language used. Grass-roots workers may be referred to as 'troops', committee members as 'chaps'. It is decided to 'play to touch' or the budget is 'front loaded' (a term usually used in connection with articulated lorries). Management meetings often begin with lengthy discussions about yesterday's play in the current football match or test match. Sometimes it is necessary to do more than talk about sport. Head hunters have even been known to enquire about a possible recruit's track record in the college sports team (Beth Thomas, 1987). Feeding in to this 'public school' culture is the pressure over the last few years from the government for local authorities to become more 'business like', which has resulted in business men who know nothing about the personal social services being brought in to senior management posts accompanied by more management jargon – 'business plans', 'marketing strategies', 'performance indicators' – and values and models of management that are more appropriate to running a supermarket in a competitive environment than being applied in the personal social services. Strangely the businessmen seem not to have noticed that the vast majority of their 'customers' are women, many of them black. If they had, they might have been expected to modify their 'product' accordingly.

This male culture is an alien one for women managers; for one woman on her own it is an uphill task to challenge and change. Even with sizeable numbers of women managers it is a hard one to tackle, but it is also a fundamental one. We are not fighting a war, we are not playing a game, we are providing a service to people with human needs who are often the victims of these same competitive values in the outside world. Women, of course, are considered to have no place on the battlefield, or the rugby pitch, or in the boardroom. They should be at home minding the children, laundering the sportsgear whiter than white, or in the office supporting the 'troops' by typing the letters and making the tea. Perhaps it is not surprising, therefore, that so many men are apparently incapable of relating to women as colleagues or sisters. They prefer to relate to them as servants, mothers, daughters or potential sex partners.

The following examples of inappropriate behaviour by men colleagues will be familiar to all women managers:

● Attending meetings with a junior male colleague or answering his phone and automatically being assumed by other people to be his secretary, or even occasionally a 'hostess' or 'floozie'.

● Having contributions to meetings ignored or talked over, which are subsequently often taken up by men as if they were their ideas.

● Having to deal with men who can only relate to women in authority aggressively or seductively. 'By being a powerful woman I present a problem to powerful men, who feel threatened and react aggressively' (Christine Walby, 1987).

● Being the only woman in all male groups which 'close ranks, have in jokes and discuss important matters in the pub or gents' (Christine Walby, 1987).

● Being expected to take on a domestic role, for example, pouring tea at meetings (this even happened to a woman chief officer at a Directors' board meeting).

● Being overlooked in favour of a junior male colleague. 'An experienced and senior female group leader (in a residential centre for adolescents) organises a camping trip for staff and boys. Her male line manager, however, continually seeks and gives information to a junior male care officer also involved in the camp. When the group is away the same line manager phones and specifically asks to speak to the male care officer about "how things are going"' (Marian Radford, Jim Rose and Giovanna Staniscia, 1988).

● Introducing a black woman at a conference as 'the woman with the sexiest topic on the agenda' (Dee Springer, 1989).

● Having to play organisational politics, which are often vicious and nasty – real 'war games'.

● Being accused of being emotional when expressing strong views.

● Being considered incapable of exercising control; for example, over adolescent males.

● Being expected to work an 80-hour week, which is regarded as commitment, management strength and effectiveness (SSI, 1989).

● Being exposed to sexual innuendo (a woman chief officer's sexuality was questioned by fellow male chief officers as a way of belittling her).

● Being bullied or pressured into taking on more work by implication of personal inadequacy or lack of commitment to the job.

● Being accused of lack of commitment to the job if domestic arrangements intrude into work.

● Being patronised by men in more senior positions.

These are the sorts of situations which women managers are exposed to on a daily basis. They are a few examples of the techniques used by men, deliberately or unconsciously, in order to exercise control and hang on to their power.

Some women are able to laugh at such ploys, or to feel sorry for the depths to which the perpetrators sink. However, for many women, working with men is painful. It hurts to be dismissed, exploited or undermined. Women in management often feel battered by their organisation, with more investment seeming to be made in their failing than in their succeeding.

Common dilemmas

We will now examine a little more closely some of the common dilemmas faced by women managers.

Most managers spend a high proportion of their time in meetings. The experience of women in meetings with men are remarkably similar. Women who have no problems at all in communicating with other women suddenly find in meeting with male colleagues or bosses that they are not being 'heard', and feel that they are not on the same 'wavelength'. They often blame themselves for not knowing enough or not being an effective communicator, but it is significant that almost all women have similar experiences. We will give three examples:

● A woman makes a point at a meeting; it is either ignored, talked over, put down or interrupted. The same point is later made by a man as if it is his idea; it is listened to and discussed. In a conversation about this phenomenon a colleague joked that she was often tempted to 'wear a beard and speak into a microphone'. A member of WISE (Women in Social Work Education) remarked 'They hear it enough to swipe the idea!'

● A man talks at length in a confident manner. The people present do not understand what he is talking about. No one challenges him.

● A woman decides to remain silent about something she feels strongly about but is unsure whether she can express herself 'adequately'.

Communication

One of the ways people exercise power over each other is through speech and language. Research shows that in discussions in mixed groups of women and men, men exercise power in a number of ways, even if they are in a minority. Firstly, they talk more than women. One of the authors has noticed that every year the three to five men in a group of twenty-five students always dominate discussions. Martin Willis (1990) observed that in a meeting with an equal number of women and men, the men made ninety-eight contributions, the women forty. In addition, the men tended to speak for longer than the women.

Men in mixed gender groups also control the subject matter: 'I don't think this sort of discussion leads anywhere'; 'Let's get back to the point'. They regularly interrupt other people, being happy to compete for space to talk. Women are uncomfortable in such an environment, preferring to take turns in an orderly way (SSI, 1989).

In their study, Don Zimmerman and Candice West (1975) found that 98 per cent of interruptions in mixed gender conversations were made by men. Because women usually allow themselves to be interrupted this is a successful technique for men to gain more air time for themselves and to silence women. Men, however, usually do not allow interruptions: 'May I finish?' Another technique used by men is to speak forcefully, confidently and loudly, which often gives the impression that they know more than they do. This style often has the effect of carrying others along with them or deterring possible disagreement. Lower pitched voices help this process along. Women often retain 'little girl' voices which detract from the weight of what they are saying. Martin Willis (1990) noted that the men in the group he observed tended to express an authoritative opinion or judgement rather than ask questions or give a personal point of view. 'Women's statements were not normally followed up by the next speaker, while men spoke in a way which effectively demanded an immediate response' (SSI, 1989). Men also try to control conversations by criticising the style of a woman's contribution in order to discredit the content: 'Why do you have to be so emotional (or hysterical or aggressive or irrational)?'

It is ironical that emotions, which are inevitably a feature of work in the personal social services, are thought by men to have no role in the workplace. Women often 'want to talk about the feelings that are raised by an issue, which male colleagues tend to discount as an inappropriate or over-emotional response'.

In private life men often make the same criticisms. However, increasingly, women are becoming highly critical of men for their 'emotional illiteracy'. It is becoming recognised by some men as well as by women that men are afraid of expressing emotions which may make them feel weak. It is interesting that the only areas of emotion that men routinely allow themselves are sexual passion and anger. Both these are areas in which they can usually exercise their power to control the situation.

As Dale Spender (1985) says, 'When women do not speak in terms which are acceptable to men they do not get a proper hearing. Women are "queried", interrupted, their opinions discounted, their contribution devalued in virtually all the mixed sex conversations I have taped.'

The use of sexist language also negates women. Words such as 'manpower', 'chairman', 'he' and 'him' being used when referring either to mixed groups of people or to women only, exclude women and are offensive to many. It is interesting that words have been changed to accommodate men, for example, 'matron' to 'officer in charge', but attempts to change language to avoid excluding women are sometimes condemned as petty or unnecessary.

Men are often skilled in the use of jargon, which also has the effect of excluding others. 'Management speak' (sometimes called 'bullshitting') picked up from management training or textbooks is an effective ploy for making mysterious something essentially simple, or communicating exclusively with others who have learned the same jargon.

Women usually prefer to communicate in more informal ways: in meetings, for example, getting rid of the tables, addressing people directly rather than through the chair, and valuing the content of a contribution rather than the status of the contributor.

It is interesting that scoring points, putting others down, interrupting and holding the floor, are regarded by men as acceptable ways of behaving. These tactics are usually designed to enhance personal standing, exclude uncomfortable issues and win other people round to a particular viewpoint to the exclusion of others.

We need to ask ourselves whether these are acceptable techniques to use in managing a personal social service. Should we not be concerned with looking for the best solution in the interests of consumers, therefore ensuring that all points of view are heard and given consideration?

Women often have important skills to bring to this process: willingness to listen to other people's points of view and to build on them; a commitment to provide a good service; techniques to encourage participation; and supportiveness to other women. Most women need to develop skills of persistence: for example, a refusal to be interrupted or talked over. Watching discussion programmes on television can give ideas about how to do this.

Chairing a meeting is a particularly good opportunity to influence the tone of the meeting, to control those who are hogging the space, to ensure that others get heard by offering opportunities and support, and to ask for explanations of jargon.

Training

Most women managers want management training (Ruth Popplestone, forthcoming), but for many it is an alienating experience. Not only are most management trainers and participants on courses men, but the whole ethos usually supports men and devalues women (SSI, 1989). The models presented and the style of training, the language and examples relate to men and their experiences. The emphasis on rationality and the concrete may devalue skills and perceptions related to emotions, which thus devalue women's skills. Many women benefit from women-only training, but some women consider that this marginalises them even further. Management training should be provided in a way that recognises that it is important for everyone to develop their own style of management, rather than conform to a predetermined model (SSI, 1991).

Stress

Being ignored, undermined, put down and devalued is stressful, and of course stress is, in any case, an everyday fact of life in personal social services work: by its very nature the work is stressful. Increasing demands and diminishing resources to meet them further increase the inherent stress, particularly for people who really care about the quality of the service. In the late 1980s, there were repeated calls for employers to set up staff care services, particularly in connection with the increasing incidence of violence towards staff. Very few responded to those calls.

Researchers have turned their attention towards stress amongst managers in general, and more recently women managers. Marilyn Davidson and Cary Cooper (1983) found that women managers are subjected to a greater number of work-related pressures than are their male counterparts; for example, being the token woman, lack of role models, feelings of isolation, strains of coping with prejudice, and discrimination. However, successful women managers consider that their ability to handle stress is one factor in their success.

Reconciling their two roles, paid work and domestic, is, of course, another major stress factor for women. Not surprisingly, women managers with children find themselves less able to relax than do men when they return home from work. Indeed, coming home is often another stress for them. At all levels of management, tiredness ranked as the stress symptom most common to women managers, followed by depression and anxiety (Marilyn Davidson and Cary Cooper, 1983). Overload is identified as the leading cause of stress, although Cary Cooper (1991) is now saying that most stress can be traced to poor management.

Women managers are far more susceptible to stress linked with private life (Marilyn Davidson and Cary Cooper, 1983). The most common source is the dilemma about whether and when to have children; many women experience a conflict between establishing their career and having children before it is too late. The second most common factor is their experience of the conflicting activities of running a home and a career: 90 per cent of the women managers studied in a Social Services

Department experienced conflicts between work and personal life (Ruth Popplestone, forthcoming). This involves the desire to fit work around men, children and dependent adults to avoid disturbing them. Women often have to 'juggle' priorities to meet the demands of others on their time. Many working women experience guilt about not being more available to act as unpaid carers. As we have already mentioned, having a wife and children lends respectability to a man's career and often implies a high level of practical and emotional support. For most women, far from a husband and children providing support in their careers, they are likely to imply the direct opposite (Nigel Nicholson and Michael West, 1988). Single women and lesbians experience other stresses concerned with the lack of social acceptability of their lifestyles. In 'dual career' families which have been studied, the women's careers always took second place to those of their husbands (Rhona Rapoport, 1976).

One way of reducing stress is to share it with others and get support. As we have already seen, women usually get very little support or caring from other people, although they are expected to, and usually do, supply it in good measure to others. Networking is a means of getting and giving support and bringing influence to bear in conjunction with other people. We will be examining this in more detail in Chapter 10.

In this chapter we have examined what it is like to be a woman manager in the personal social services. We have given a number of examples of real-life situations which women have encountered, and identified some common dilemmas which women managers face.

8

Managing with Style

The significance of style

In previous chapters we looked at how the control strand of
personal social services work, particularly management, has
become increaingly associated with men by emphasising
certain qualities and skills that they are thought to possess.
Such qualities are often translated into behaviour which is
contradictory to the qualities thought necessary in people
doing caring work. Organisations often appear polarised by
these two sets of values. In this chapter we will be examining
some questions raised for women about management style.

Management style is rarely discussed in detail in management literature (Charles Handy (1985) allocates three pages to
it in a chapter on leadership); yet for many women managers,
style is a fundamental component of effective managing. Its
absence as a topic for research and debate is significant: as
long as most managers are men, and most writers and theorists
of management are men, style can be taken for granted, for it
will inevitably and unquestioningly be male. However, as
women take on management positions, or think about their
careers, questions about style arise. Questions such as:

- Is there a female management style?
- How far is my management style affected by my being
  both a manager and a woman?
- If I seek promotion will my management style become
  more like that of other senior managers? (Do they manage
  the way they do because of their seniority or because most
  of them, if not all of them, are men)?

Following these questions, other, more tentative, ones arise:

● Am I really managing in the way I would choose, or do I often have to manage in the way that the organisation expects me to?
● Am I losing something intrinsic about who I am and how I see staff and the service we offer?

Often these questions remain unspoken, for who can women managers ask? Isolated women managers may doubt the validity of their questions and even of their experience: 'Well, perhaps it's a silly thing to be thinking'; 'not all women are like me, and men vary, so maybe there isn't such a thing as "women's style" of management'.

As long as these questions about style remain unasked and hidden, they fail to be discussed in books or on courses; or they become transformed into topics such as 'leadership', or 'effectiveness' (for example in the Open University course 'The Effective Manager'). Such transformation does not encompass or do justice to the complexity of managing that concerns women. 'Style', as women use the term, seems to be a holistic concept that permits elements such as teamwork, decision-making, use of power and authority, leadership, interpersonal skills and so on to be interwoven within it.

So the idea of management style, despite its absence from most management books, is important for women, not only because it allows for this holistic approach to managing, but also because it raises questions about MANagement and thereby organisational cultures which have sustained masculine practice. Understanding the part organisational culture plays in management style is an important part of unravelling the way women manage.

Organisational culture and management style

The role of 'manager of others' is a relatively recent phenomenon in organisations (Wendy Hirsch and Stephen Bevan, 1988). It became necessary only when large clusters of people started working together to achieve an agreed end and their work needed 'organising'. Models for the role of manager came from other clusterings of large numbers of people, as in the armed services, the Church and public schools. What is significant about these groupings is that they tended to be:

rule bound – and therefore with systems for punishing rule breaking;
hierarchic – with clearly defined roles, and rules about how seniority is to be achieved;
competitive;
concerned with winning (a place in heaven if not on earth); and
run by men (even convents were usually answerable to men such as archdeacons and popes).

The systems of recruitment and promotion, of rules and punishment, of ideology and behaviour, have all left traces that can be found in many contemporary organisations. Marilyn Loden (1985) describes them as a 'culture of masculinism'. For her, the significant features are:

Operating style   = competitive
Organisational structure = hierarchy
Basic objective   = winning
Problem solving style   = rational
Key characteristics   = high control
                            strategic
                            analytic

The similarities between her list and common characteristics of large groupings such as armies, the Church and public schools is immediately apparent. It would seem, therefore, that many of our organisations which require 'managing' have been imbued with the 'culture of masculinism' because of the history of management and because it is men who have done the managing.

Another way of understanding the 'culture' of organisations and how this is then reflected in the management style and ethos is to look to origins of the key words themselves. As we saw in Chapter 4 the word *management* comes from the Italian word *maneggiare*, which, roughly translated, means 'handling things', especially horses. Again, there is a military context – this time the cavalry. Phrases that reflect this can also be found in organisations: 'getting the bit between the teeth'; 'being in the saddle'; 'gaining one's spurs'; 'taking over the reins' are all expressions about taking control of things and/or people.

The other source for the word *management*, *menager*, a French word, means 'careful use' and is concerned with housekeeping. The diffuseness of housekeeping means that its components are harder to identify than those of organisations. Housekeeping:

requires a wide range of practical, interpersonal and negotiating skills, which can be called on simultaneously;
is concerned with keeping others in good physical and emotional repair;
requires an ability to predict future needs;
is largely invisible; and
is mainly undertaken by women.

In the personal social services, like many other organisations, the pervasive culture of 'masculinism', combined with the predominance of white men, can make the management arena a 'hostile environment' for women, particularly black women, to work in. It is this, combined with the strong sense that management is not just about control, winning, rationality and so on, that prompts the questions:

● Does it have to be like that?
● Do I have to be like that?
● What might a different management culture be like?

As some women, some of the time, ask these questions and try to manage in a different way, they create the possibility of a different style and culture in the organisation. It is to this glimpse of a different style and culture that we now turn.

Women's style

Diffences in management style between women and men have been shown to exist by research in both the private and public sectors (Rosemary Dinnage, 1989; Ruth Eley, 1986; Marilyn Loden, 1985; Judi Marshall, 1984). The writer of this chapter, Julia Phillipson, and her colleague Maggie Riley, have developed three different ways of analysing style on their self-development programmes for women managers:

● Women are asked to pick a word which they think best describes their management style.
● Women are asked to think of concrete examples of their work as managers which are then analysed for similarities and differences.
● By analysing the use of power and how women perceive it.

Readers might like to try these methods for unravelling style for themselves. However, they are not the only methods. Style, as already suggested, seems to be an encompassing concept for women managers, so there are potentially lots of other pathways to exploring and understanding style!

Style in a word

What word or short phrase would you use to describe your style as a manager? (If you are not yet a manager but are thinking of becoming one, imagine yourself a manager with a team and think how your imaginary team members would describe you.)

Here are some of the words that other women have suggested typify their style:

Good with muddle   Open   Non-combative

Innovative   Firm sense of quality   Bridge-building

Responsive   Approachable   Humorous   Valuing

Incorporative   Person-centred   Flexible

Communicative   Honest   Female   Irrepressible

Decisive   Capable   Rewarding   Enabling   Fun-loving

Fluid   Persuasive   Supportive   Caring

Flamboyant   Committed   Consultative   Strong

Some words have appeared repeatedly during this activity, particularly 'responsive', 'caring', 'committed' and 'honest'. Some different words are thought of each time, suggesting both recurring themes and uniqueness in women's style.

There are other significant things about the words that are chosen, which help illuminate women's management style further.

The words describe both 'being' and 'doing'

For women managers how they 'are' is interwoven with, and is as important as, what they do, or how they behave. Management has mainly been described as a 'doing' activity by management theorists (for example, John Hughes, 1988). In practice, too, there is a current preoccupation with doing, and with outcome. Process assumes less importance. This is not the case for many women, as is shown by words such as 'bridge-building', 'communicative', and 'consultative'.

The words may well reflect the way women are currently 'grown', which will be fundamental to their style

Women are expected to be 'caring', 'committed', 'responsive', 'flexible', 'good with muddle' and so on. This raises the question 'Are women managers just being and doing what is expected of women?' This question raises another – 'Do managers have to be or do something different from how they are as "people", or how they are as women?' Social work literature has long tussled with whether managers in social work need to be different from how they are as basic grade workers – and most workers are women. Are men promoted because they bring something different, which is seen as the 'stuff of management'? Wendy Hirsch and Stephen Bevan's research (1988) would suggest that this has been the case.

*The words could apply equally well to working with service users
as with colleagues*

The words in themselves are not necessarily positive or negative

Being enabling may not always be a good thing – challenging
may on occasion be more appropriate than enabling with
regard to, for example, racism or sexism; flexibility may not be
appropriate in circumstances which require decisiveness.

However, most women were very positive about the lists
they generated together, seeing these attributes as valuable for
staff, users and the organisations and as being rooted in a set
of values that they also tried to espouse as managers. These
are highly important aspects of management practice, but they
have not been the ones that have been emphasised in
management training or in the criteria for promotion (Ruth
Popplestone, 1980).

*Most women identified with most of the words, regardless of
position, age, ethnicity, background*

However, the extent to which the women were able to be and
act in the style that they emphasised varied. Being flamboyant
may be more difficult if you are the only woman in the senior
management team where you are already very conspicuous –
on the other hand, it may be a way of remaining different!
Bridge-building was a word chosen by a black woman
manager who worked in the voluntary sector, which itself
necessitates liaison. However, the isolation and pain of racism
as well as the strengths learnt through combating it may well
mean that for such women bridge-building is both visionary
and a daily survival task.

*The words 'fit' with those aspects that research suggests typifies
many women managers*

Marilyn Loden (1985) identified eight areas where she felt that
women managed in a different way:

● Use of power – women tend to focus on empowering
others rather than on personal power acquisition.

● Problem solving – women use their intuitively based knowledge in conjuction with 'rational' information. Rather than being the traditionally valued 'single minded', women are 'multi-minded'. (A word developed on the courses in response to the women saying that they were often told that they weren't single minded enough! Recording and reviewing the one word women choose to describe their style provides some clues as to their own perception of key features of their style. Looking at examples of managing is a second way.)

● Interpersonal skills – women bring and use a wide range of skills, such as listening and empathy.

● Team work and participative management – women tend to be team-focused, not merely organisation-focused, and use team members' skills in managing.

● Standard setting and risk taking – women are deeply concerned with the quality of service; they also have to be twice as good to be seen as competent. Taken together, these factors mean that women expect and demand a lot of themselves and the service provided – they may be seen as 'tough'. Women take risks to sustain or improve the service.

● Managing diversity, stress and boundaries – women generally give this prime consideration and do it well for other staff; they are not always able to do it so well for themselves.

● Handling conflict– women attempt to find win-win solutions through collaboration or assertive negotiations rather than 'scoring' gains at the expense of others.

● Pitching in and professional development – women will tend to join in if a job needs doing, even if it is not officially part of their role. They are also concerned to seek development for themselves and other women. In both these ways they challenge hierarchic ways of organising.

Style in practice

Think of examples of your management practice where gender differences seem evident. The following brief was given to women.

Think of times when:

● After seeing a male colleague in action you thought, 'I wouldn't have managed the situation in that way.'
● Someone calls into question how you have managed something such as a meeting, or relations with a colleague or a team member. It is possible that how you behaved, or what you said, was challenged – usually for being of the wrong quantity, ('you are giving her too much time'), or the wrong quality ('you need to be tougher'), or both ('you need to speak up more in meetings'). In some way you have been found deficient; a judgement you may or may not have accepted, but is likely to have made you ask 'would they have said that if I were a man?'
● You have wondered whether how you were responded to was to do primarily with the fact that you are a woman.

Or perhaps you can think of managers you have had and what gender differences, if any, there were in their style.

The following are some examples given by women managers, which are then unravelled to tease out 'style' components.

Example 1

A team leader was rung in the middle of the night and told by a male colleague to 'get your F-ing arse up out of bed and come and help me'. He was drunk and sounded both desperate and aggressive. She knew he had both a drink and personal problems. When she later discussed her response with her male line manager, she was told 'what he needs is a slap on the wrist', and also that 'men will drink'. Her request not to supervise him any more was taken as a sign of inadequacy on her part.

Unravelling some elements of her style

● Feeling responsible – the woman felt 'I can't do nothing' and therefore went to find him, despite being upset and angry at his behaviour towards her.

● Empathy - 'I knew he was in trouble and I knew that he must be feeling really awful.'
● Getting to grips with the real problems – 'I wanted his drink problem to be tackled, not treated as something all men do. Instead it was covered over.'
● Honesty – 'I felt our relationship was such that I could no longer supervise him fairly.'

Example 2

A big mailing of publicity about a new service was planned. Knowing this, and the fact that the administrative staff were already very overworked, a woman manager booked time into her diary to help with filling envelopes. When it was all done she bought the staff flowers.

Unravelling some elements of her style

● Empathy – 'I knew how busy the staff were and also how boring it is to fill endless envelopes.'
● Pitching in – 'I felt the least I could do was to take my turn and do some of the mail-out with them.'
● Recognising and rewarding work – 'I think it is very important to let people know that you appreciate the work they do, perhaps especially when it is boring and undertaken willingly.'
● Making time and space for celebrations – 'As a team we try to find lots of reasons for celebrating – birthdays. special events, getting to the end of another week.'

Example 3

A senior woman manager was attending a monthly management meeting in which she was the only woman. A number of aspects concerned her about the way the meeting was handled, such as the games playing; the kinds of items that were put forward for the agenda; the way policy decisions were made without full consideration of the ramifications for staff and users; and the remoteness of the discussions from the reality of users. Having analysed the dynamics of the meeting, she made a conscious decision to start talking about individual service users, and to talk about their lives; how the services were or weren't meeting their needs; and what the implication of changes might mean for them.

Unravelling some elements of her style

● A preoccupation with service provided – 'I felt as if everyone had become completely out of touch and they were really using the meetings to bolster their own position.'

● Attending to the unique – 'I made sure that I knew what was happening to individuals we were working with. It seemed important that in the meeting and in our discussions we kept sight of people as individuals – not just as a group for whom we had "targets".'

● Risk-taking – 'Talking about individuals was not part of the expected behaviour at this meeting; I ran the risk of being ignored, or of having what I said treated as an irrelevant interruption to the real work!'

● Working counter-culture – 'I am always having to make decisions about whether to behave in the same way as everyone else; in this instance I decided not to, to see what happened – whether I could make a difference.'

● Sticking with values – 'I believe we should be concerned with the quality of the service that we offer, as well as with budgets, committee papers and so on. I felt I needed to put up a marker for that, and keep on doing it when necessary.'

Examples of men's behaviour can also be used to illustrate differences.

Example 4

A woman manager was called in by her male line manager and told confidentially that in the plans for reorganisation it was not clear if she would have a post. Her distress was ignored, and the line manager was not able to provide answers to her questions about the time scale, salaries of new posts and so on. The line manager did confirm that he had got the post he wanted.

Her male partner, a management consultant in the private sector, did not think the line manager would have behaved in this way towards a man.

Her decision to take the matter up was seen as her being 'difficult'.

Example 5

A senior woman, one of only two women at her level, described how her male line manager had told her, 'I really feel I can talk to you, and share my problems.' Flattered at first, and taking it as an indication that her judgement was respected, she found that her supervision time was spent focusing on his issues. She later discovered that he had said the same thing to her woman colleague, claiming to both that each was the only one he could talk to.

Example 6

A woman manager described how when her line manager arrived in the morning he asked her how she was. If she said 'fine' he stayed to chat, but if she started to say anything about not feeling so good he vanished as fast as he could.

These examples suggest that women are good managers whilst men are not – clearly this is not always the case! What many of the examples highlight is that sexism is present in some male managers' dealings with women colleagues and this is an important part of their style. Women managers too can adopt a 'male style' of managing and act oppressively towards other women, not only in matters relating to gender but also with regard to race and sexual orientation.

Same words, different meanings

Many women seek promotion because they want to influence the way services are developed and delivered. In order to be influential and bring about change they will need to acquire and use power.
BUT

● Women who act powerfully are liable to fail the daily 'real woman' test: real women are . . . kind, good listeners, concerned for others, don't throw their weight around and so on. Hence good managers are powerful, but good women aren't, so what are good women managers to be?
● If you have experienced being put down, trivialised, shrunk, and ignored by others more 'powerful' than yourself, (including by other women), how do you come to terms with trying to become more powerful or being expected to be more powerful?
● If as women we want to make a difference we have to resolve these contradictions:

how to be powerful and treat others with respect;
how to be powerful and not damage; and
how to be powerful and pass our own internal 'good woman' test.

How women conceptualise power and how they choose or are able to use it, is a critical dimension of their management style. A brainstorm on the word 'power' is sometimes a good place to start. What follows are the words one group of women generated. There were many obviously negative words such as: demeaning, oppressive, force, destructive, threatened, frightening, corrupting, dangerous. (Words such as strong, forceful, pushing also appeared.)

Then there were clearly positive words such as: creative, buzz, knowledge, making things happen, energy, influence.

Reframing

In discussion, what became apparent was that whilst words such as 'strong', 'forceful', 'decisive', 'pushing', may describe negatively-impacting power, women may be these things in different ways from men.

For example, one woman described recognising a strength in herself as being an ability 'to be brave enough to speak out about the impossibilities' rather than 'pretending' things were possible. This was particularly important when trying to juggle with inadequate resources. Another women pointed out that being able to recognise personal uncertainty and vulnerabilities were strengths that she and many other women possessed. In addition, an ability to deal with ambiguity and uncertainty were also strengths that the women recognised in themselves.

This suggested that our commonsense definitions of strength as to do with muscle-power, toughness and firmness were in themselves lop-sided and male definitions.

Women reconceptualised strength

A similar reframing took place in relation to 'forceful'. Force, for many women, is synonymous with hectoring, bullying, aggression and harassment and was not a way of being that they wanted to adopt. But there were many things about which the women felt strongly, that they knew about through experience, through listening, through collecting evidence. When these strong feelings were transformed into conviction, this became a different kind of force. Having conviction means women are often a force for positive change (see Natasha Josefowitz, 1986).

Power itself is reframed into empowerment. Power can mean 'to be able'; empowerment is about being part of making others able. A striking feature of many women's management style, as Ruth Eley's research (1986) and our own work also shows (Julia Phillipson and Maggie Riley, 1990) is the emphasis that many women place on developing other staff through enabling, supervision, shared decision-making and so on. This is very different from the male style of appropriation: going it alone, or telling others what to do rather than helping them develop their own solutions (see Alistair White, 1989).

As women conceptualise and reframe power:

● they challenge stereotypes about what effective management is;
● they highlight the way language is itself structured by gender and the way key words may need redefining; and
● they confirm the way women manage differently.

Understanding style

These three pathways into style suggest that there are many dimensions to women's style, in terms of behaviour, thinking processes, value orientation and commitments. However, as well as separating style into its components, it is also important to see it as a whole, even as women seem to use it as a unifying concept about managing.

A strand that seems to run through all the dimensions of women's style and which may be part of what makes it a whole is that of connectedness. Women appear to take with them in their management role a sense of connectedness to:

● known individuals such as team members, colleagues, often other women;
● others who may not be known individually, such as service users;
● time; and
● thought and feeling processes.

The significance of connectedness to others is revealed in women's preference for teamwork and collaborative working, in their 'feeling responsible' and empathy for others as well as in their tendency to 'pitch in'. The decision to seek promotion into senior management can be affected by a recogniton of the isolation and lack of connection that many senior women experience.

As Jalna Hanmer and Daphne Statham (1988) have shown, there is also a sense of connectedness with service users who are themselves (apart from in probation) predominantly women.

A sense of connectedness through time is also apparent in the way that many women manage. Much of management is about planning and taking action; it is often about change. What many women seem to carry with them is a sense of continuity between the past, the present and the future. This is often revealed in women's tendency to ask 'why?' and 'what for?' questions when change is demanded – not because they are change blockers or petty (as they are often accused), but rather because they carry a concern for the repercussions of possible changes. 'How will this affect others?'; 'Is it the best way?' are questions that spring out of a sense of connectedness with people and with time.

Problem-understanding and problem-solving are also important aspects of managing. Being able to connect intuitive understanding gained through empathy, an ability to read nonverbal communication,and personal experience with factual and 'objective' information can give women access to much more complex problem-solving skills. These abilities and skills when mixed with abilities of women managers to draw on team resources further adds to this!

So the various elements of women's style are themselves connected and the facet of connectedness runs through them. Trying to identify and adopt a style of management that is grounded in connectedness with who they are and how they function as women is fundamental when management in organisations is so 'masculine'.

Debating the difference

A sense of connectedness may be one of the unifying features of many women's style, and may be an important facet of their difference from many men. Neither men nor women are, however, working to compulsory blueprints and it may be more helpful to draw a continuum of behaviour and approaches and to consider where most women and men would come on that continuum, and what the choices and constraints about a place on the continuum are, and whether they are different for women than for men, or in different settings, or for different kinds of women. Margaret Richards (1990) offers two versions of models of management that managers might hold. They can be seen as such a continuum.

Management as	Management as
Power over people/resources	Empowerment
Pre-occupation with policies/ procedures as defined by management	Listening, and consulting users and all staff about needs
Quality control defined by management	Idea of quality rooted in users' views
Rationing. Saying 'no'	Motivating for creative changes to work processes
Emphasis on outcome via monitoring, performance indicators and so on	Emphasis on staff development, feedback
Managers' right to manage, telling people	Negotiating, exploring possibilities
Maintaining 'clarity'	Tolerating ambiguity and uncertainty

Psychological and sociological theories would suggest that the way our worlds are gendered – through language, through societal expectations of women and of men; through the differing impact of fiscal and social policies and so on, will all play their part in why we are the way we are. As we have seen, they affect the work that we choose to do and that is open to us; they will affect the values and commitments we bring to work. The gendering of society has meant that management has been largely a white male preserve for men to organise so that it reflects their concerns, their way of thinking and behaving, and their lifestyle. When women move into management they bring values, behaviour, commitments and ways of being that are grounded in how they are as women, although how they are as women will itself be diverse and be mediated through race, and class and sexual orienation as well as through gender.

The issue for many women managers becomes whether to move towards that side of the continuum that fits the 'culture of masculinism'. For some women this does not pose a dilemma; some will state 'I've never had any problems (with men) – I don't see what the problem is'. Others will recognise that there is some kind of a problem for some women, but will say of themselves 'I've never had any problems, I've had a man's career' –usually meaning that they have wanted and been able to obtain senior positions. Yet other women move upwards in the management hierarchy and have a sense that they are in danger of being transformed or having to be transformed in order to survive. One woman manager said that she felt as if she were being 'bent out of shape'; others speak of their concern about getting used to the 'macho style' and hardly noticing it any more. For those women who are very isolated in senior management the pressure to 'fit' is extreme. The video by Ora Fant *et al.* (1980), 'A Tale of "O", On Being Different' demonstrates the extra performance pressures and the spotlight that such women, or other numerically rare people, are put under. Such pressures can result in joining in with the prevailing norms. The disappointment of other women, their feeling that they have been 'sold out', may act as a further incentive to an isolated woman to feel that she will do better to 'join the boys' than stay loyal to the other women. Failure can become a pervasive possibility in such circumstances.

It is no wonder, then, that the style in which they manage is of concern to many women. To manage in a male way is to have to become something that they are not – like men; but to manage in a different way – like a woman – is to run the risk of being spotted as different, and of being ignored, ridiculed, or overworked. To live with the sexism so prevalent in organisations on a daily basis is wearing and demoralising in the extreme. Black women managers also have to survive the envy of many white women and the exploitation of the black managers as 'super experts'. The fact that many women are recruited because they are told the organisation wants something different: either numerically (we need more black women, more lesbians, more women with disabilities); or of quality (we need your humanising touch) makes the contradictions the more bizarre.

As women we need to create spaces in organisations where we can manage in a way that feels right. We need to create times when we can share the contradictions and the dilemmas of managing as women and learn how we have unravelled the contradictions and worked with the dilemmas. We need to name what we do, celebrate what we do well, and manage with style.

9

Power

In the previous chapter we looked at how some women have learned to reconceptualise power and to use it in a positive way to empower rather than to dominate and control other people. In this chapter we will look at power from a slightly different angle – how it is used and how it is abused. Because it is so frequently abused, power is often regarded as a dirty word by those who think they do not possess it.

Women often complain about feelings of powerlessness, but we saw in the last chapter that when they begin to reflect on the different aspects of power and their relation to them, they recognise that they do sometimes feel powerful, and that they can identify with the positive aspects of powerfulness.

It is vital that women managers do learn how to handle power constructively because it is part of the management task and an everyday fact of life in organisations.

Power in organisations

In all organisations there are individuals and groups competing for influence or resources, there are differences of opinion and of values, conflicts of priorities and of goals. There are pressure groups and lobbies, cliques and cabals, rivalries and contests, clashes of personality and bonds of alliance. (Charles Handy, 1986)

What often comes as a shock to women managers is the ruthless way in which many men exercise power in organisations, which of course affects their behaviour towards colleagues. One of the best-known theorists on organisations unwittingly points up this difference in behaviour:

> By the age of maturity man has acquired or developed the habits of competition, is a creature used to aggression; the ways of managing that state, of channelling its energies and resolving its problems is the art or the science of politics in organisations. (Charles Handy, 1986)

The use of the word 'man' in this paragraph is significant. The writer does not mean his remarks to refer only to men. He uses the word in the sense of 'people'. What he fails to recognise is that what he says does not, in fact, apply to women. By the age of maturity women have acquired the skills of co-operation, which they have learned through years of training to be aware of and fit in with the needs of others. Their aggression, often directed against themselves in the form of self doubt and lack of confidence, could flow into constructive work.

However, women do have to use a lot of energy to avoid being the victims of male aggression, to protect themselves and others from its effects, and to understand the power games which are being played. The alternative for women is to 'join the club', behave aggressively themselves and become an active participant in the games. If they choose this course of action, they are then criticised from all quarters and become the proverbial 'dragons', and not 'real women'. (Margaret Thatcher was described by Barbara Castle as 'the right man for the job'.) Interestingly, Charles Handy (1986) advocates the expression of feelings in order to avoid conflict. However, he dismisses this as a practical option, because 'the expression of feelings is not culturally respectable in the Anglo-Saxon tradition . . . Openness requires trust and confidence, and that only comes with a mature and effective group'. Without realising it, he is endorsing what is second nature to many women managers – expression of feelings and discussing them openly with their colleagues. He considers that 'trust, collaboration and mutual help' are rarely achieved in organisations. This is a remarkable statement, which together with his other comments indicates that he has minimal experience of working with women, and no understanding of the way they usually prefer to operate. This is also an excellent example of the way in which books on management are written by men, about men and for men, taking no account of the experience and behaviour of women.

Types of power

In order to understand women's relationship with power, it is useful to recognise various different types of power. Those most commonly identified are: the power of expertise, personal power, resource power and position power. Women usually find it easier to use and identify with the first two of these.

As we have seen, women do not usually become managers until they are very well grounded in their professional work. They prefer to be respected for their work before assuming responsibility for the work of others. On becoming managers, therefore, they tend to rely first and foremost on the power of their professional expertise; that is, their specialist knowledge, skills and qualifications, firmly grounded in practice experience.

Personal power resides in the person. It is the power people have to get on with others, the ability to persuade and to build good quality relationships. People in caring jobs rely on it all the time: the self is an important tool which they have learned to use in their work, so it is a comfortable source of power for the woman manager in the personal social services to draw on. However, as women's personal power is sometimes achieved by means of manipulation, it may be necessary for them to learn more assertive ways of using it.

Resource power derives from control of resources, be they money, equipment or supplies: for example, stationery, training and car parking spaces. The way this control is exercised makes a profound difference to those who use the resources. It varies from the manager who exercises rigid control in order to conserve the resources, to the manager who goes out of her way to meet the needs of the resource users by allocating them as flexibly as possible.

Position power is the most commonly recognised type of power and also the most commonly abused. It relates to position at work, at home and in society. This is the power with which people are vested through the formal authority of their position.

In the past, the head of the household was always assumed to be a man, and if a man resides in the house he still usually assumes the role of head, particularly if he is a husband or father. In most households there is usually no doubt about who is the most powerful person: women are usually financially dependent on men, who generally earn more or are the formal recipient of state benefits as they are deemed by the state to be responsible for supporting women, who are not allowed to claim in their own right if they live with a man.

Men also hold power by virtue of their position in society. Throughout most of recorded history it is men who have been gods, kings, rulers, popes, bishops, presidents, prime ministers, judges, generals, 'captains of industry', directors of financial institutions, scientists, recognised artists and writers. History is written as though these are the only people of importance. Women, as now, were in support and caring roles, and were rarely recognised unless they behaved like men. Indeed, until very recently, women were viewed as the property of men and still are in many parts of the world. When asked to explain why there are no women represented in history men argue that it is because women have nothing to contribute. Dale Spender (1982) comments:

> It is not that women have not played an equal part in history, but that men have written the history books and have focused on the problems of men: it is not that women have not generated religious thoughts, formulated political philosophies, explained society, written poetry or been artists, but that men have controlled the records for religion, philosophy, politics, poetry and art and they have concentrated on the contributions of men.

Men are still in control of government, religious organisations, the armed forces, the law and industry. Men direct the course of states, corporations and cultures. They control people, creatures and the environment. Every avenue to power in society is firmly in men's hands. Furthermore, white men control black people, and heterosexual men control gay men. Men own 99 per cent of the world's property, and earn 90 per cent of its wages (International Labour Organisation, 1980).

Men have been able to exercise this control over the centuries by virtue of their relative physical strength and their freedom from childbearing and childrearing. For thousands of years this has been linked to a supposed 'natural superiority' and many men behave as if they still consider this to be true. At work 'the boss' is assumed to be a man (and usually is). This gives him the right to organise other people's work and make decisions about it, sometimes including pay and promotion. And he often behaves as though it gives him many other rights, as we have seen throughout this book.

Position power symbolises superiority, even if it rests only in a higher salary, a bigger office or physical size. Although position power can be undermined, and relies on the consent of others, it has connotations of coercion and physical power. Bullying behaviour in the workplace, the home or the street carries the threat of physical violence. The physical presence of a dictatorial boss may seem coercive. Position power at work can easily be used in a coercive way because it carries with it the power to make or break other people's careers, to make people's working lives miserable, to deprive them of their jobs, to restructure, make redundant and make cuts, regardless of the human consequences.

All women have experience of position power being misused and abused. Indeed, this is what discrimination against women and others is all about, and we have given many examples of it in this book. Marilyn French (1985) considers that 'the true end of male institutions is to maintain at any cost the appearance of male control'. To this end it is of the utmost importance for men to occupy the positions of power and for their status (the appearance of control) to be emphasised and recognised. As we have seen, men tend to be much more interested in status than are women. Hence 'the most subversive acts in any institution are to . . . refuse to defer, to reject the idea of human superiority'; 'To go over the head of your boss, even to a superior who is aware of the boss's inadequacies, is unforgivable because it implies a lack of proper submission' (Marilyn French, 1985).

The power of information is usually associated with position power. If position power is abused, the dissemination of information will be strictly controlled or distorted, further disadvantaging those on the receiving end. Sexism ensures that 'information' is filtered and distorted in an attempt to keep women under control so that affairs can be organised in ways which suit men.

Before discussing women and position power further, we want to mention three other types of power. These are *negative power*, *nutrient power* and *collaborative power*.

Negative power is used to block or control, and is a way of preventing change. It often comes in the form of petty restrictions, designed to show who is in charge. Negative power is used by managers who are unsure of themselves or lack expertise. Many women suffer from being on the receiving end of attempts to block or frustrate their initiatives, which are often seen as threatening by managers who may be less competent.

Nutrient power comes from care given to another person. It is therefore used a great deal by women. It is best illustrated by the firm structure which a good parent provides for a child within a caring relationship. Nutrient power can also come from the concern which a community worker, politician, president, queen or king has for the welfare of a group of people. It is the constructive aspect of their power (Rollo May, 1972).

Collaborative power is described by Rosabeth Moss Kanter (1984) as the power necessary to create innovation and change. It cuts through the more traditional types of power by making new connections, working across boundaries, mobilising people and resources to get things done. It involves persuading rather than ordering, team building, sharing information, seeking input from others, showing sensitivity to the needs of others, and sharing rewards and recognition. Although personal social services organisations scarcely ever provide the conditions for using collaborative power to its full extent, women often use it within their own teams to innovate and produce creative work.

Many women avoid being in positions which they regard as powerful. Thus many of them are promoted into advisory or specialist posts rather than line management. If they are in a position of authority, they may avoid exercising position power. As we have seen, most women managers place a great deal of emphasis on teamwork, co-operation and consultation, giving credit to the team rather than standing on their own status or seeking personal glorification. 'Powerful' applied to a woman is usually being used in a negative sense, and there are many other words which are used in a similar way – 'ball breaker', 'castrating', 'handbagging', 'aggressive', 'dragon'. Black women often seem to exercise position power more comfortably than white women, and older people more easily than younger. Both can be less inclined to appease and to want to be liked by everyone.

Position power is extremely unappealing to most white women Because they see it abused so frequently that they can easily believe that there is no positive way of exercising it.

Abuse of power

All women are at some stage in their lives victims of the abuse of male power and have been over the centuries. This book has been concerned with the abuse of power in the workplace. As women and as carers, women are also familiar with the abuse of power in the home and in society.

Kate Painter (1991) found that one in four women between the ages of eighteen and fifty-four has been raped, and one in seven of these was raped by her husband. Most of the raped wives in the survey said they were put under psychological and emotional pressures by their husbands if they refused to have sex. These included moodiness, bad temper, verbal abuse and drunkenness. Most said they were made to feel abnormal for not wanting sex whenever their husbands did. Four out of five of the raped wives reported that rape happened frequently; 44 per cent of the marital rapes were accompanied by actual or threatened violence; and one in five of the wives was pregnant when raped.

Only in 1988 did the metropolitan police begin to intervene in 'domestic disputes' after years of pressure from the women's refuge movement. Before that men were free to attack women in private. Only in the late 1970s (Erin Pizzey, 1974) was attention first drawn to 'battered women' and their need for protection from abusing men, and only recently has rape begun to be taken seriously as violence by the courts. These changes have been brought about by pressure from feminists, who have insisted that when a woman says 'no' she means it, and that women often return to or stay with abusing men not because they enjoy it, but because they are financially dependent on them. Only in 1991 did it become legally possible to charge a husband with raping his wife (House of Lords, 1991).

A study in London of women between sixteen and twenty-one (Panos Institute, 1991) found that many of them had unwanted unprotected sex because it was easier than risking an argument with partners about using condoms. Alongside studies from other parts of the world, researchers have concluded that a lack of social and economic power means that women in many societies, including Western, have very little chance of insisting on safe sex.

Available evidence suggests that child sexual abuse is widespread and abuse within the family far more common than by other adults or strangers. Between 21 per cent and 46 per cent of women have reported being sexually abused as children (Linda Percival, 1989). Events in Cleveland and Nottingham indicated that as a society we have extreme difficulty in facing up to the extent of child sexual abuse, particularly within the family.

Women, men and the abuse of power

Because our society is so lacking in models of power being exercised positively, it is easy for people who have been abused themselves to adopt the same behaviour towards others in less powerful positions. We should not forget that we are all potential perpetrators of abuse of people who are less powerful than ourselves. White women abuse black women, heterosexual women abuse lesbians, able bodied women abuse disabled people, young people abuse old people, and people in caring jobs sometimes abuse their clients. However, all studies which have looked at the gender of abusers have found that they are overwhelmingly men: 'In all studies, it is men who appear as the adults in sexual contact with children' (Danya Glaser and Stephen Frosh, 1988).

Many women workers in the personal social services are victims of the abuse of power both at work and at home. But they are also very familiar with the effects of abuse in their role as carers. Abuse of power by individuals or the system underpins many of the day-to-day problems which the personal social services exist to deal with: poverty, child abuse, neglect of elderly people, children and mentally ill people; inadequate funding (for example, for community care) exacerbates these problems: 'Because women routinely experience the abuse of power, women carers have a 'rich resource for understanding the dilemmas, strengths and resources of their clients' (Daphne Statham, 1990).

As carers in the home, too, women spend much of their time comforting, supporting and bolstering others to enable them to face abusive behaviour at school, at work and in the street. The effects of the abuse of power is part of the fabric of women's lives.

It is disturbing that men, the very group of people in society who perpetrate most of the abuse which results in women requiring intervention from the personal social services, are themselves in positions of power in those organisations. As we have seen in this book, those employed in the personal social services are no strangers to abusing their power in the workplace. At the time of writing, several men in responsible positions in community homes have been found guilty of both sexual and physical abuse of children in care and of staff for whom they are responsible (Ian Katz and David Brindle, 1991; also Frances Rickford, 1991). We do not know how often such men abuse the women and children of their own families, but some of them undoubtedly do. Can we trust a group of people who are so inclined to abuse their power to make sound decisions on behalf of the victims of abuse?

Men and abuse

Some of the people who seek to help men who have abused women or children have recorded how surprised they have been to discover that they are quite ordinary men: 'I couldn't stop being amazed that they were all regular guys, ordinary working men and average pillars of society' (Rich Snowdon, 1980).

A number of writers have also noted how reluctant these men are to take responsibility for their actions. They blame everyone but themselves. They blame their daughters: 'She was always walking around half naked, waggling her behind'; 'I was giving her some affection I thought she needed'. They blame the child's mother: 'My wife made me do it, it was her fault' (Rich Snowdon, 1980). The same reluctance to take responsibility by men as a group has been seen in some of the well-publicised child sexual abuse cases in the late 1980s.

As Mica Nava (1988) has pointed out, the two people in Cleveland who worked consistently to draw attention to the scale of sexual abuse in Cleveland were both women, Dr Marietta Higgs and Sue Richardson. Both were ignored, contradicted and ridiculed by the police, and discredited by the media. As a result, both were forced to leave their jobs. The men allied with them, Dr Geoffrey Wyatt and Mike Bishop, Director of Social Services, 'were represented . . . as wimps and weaklings in the thrall of the unseemly strength of insubordinate women' (Beatrix Campbell, 1988). This did not stop Mike Bishop from obtaining a directorship in a considerably more prestigious department shortly afterwards. Most of the other men who attracted publicity in this affair were concerned to deny the extent of the abuse (Mica Nava, 1988).

Stuart Bell, the local MP, led the campaign to protect 'innocent parents' [that is, fathers], alleging that the two women 'conspired and colluded' to exclude the police surgeon from examining the children suspected of being abused. He was supported by two other male MPs; the Revd Michael Wright (the local priest who started and led the parents' support group); and Dr Alistair Irvine, who publicly attacked Dr Higgs' professional judgement and claimed that he had been prevented by her from examining suspected cases of abuse.

Team 4, the social workers, all women, who dealt with a large group of children in Nottingham, who they maintained had been ritually abused, were consistently ridiculed and ignored in their attempts to expose the abuse (Judith Dawson, 1990). Judith Dawson was later banned from speaking about the case in public (Social Work Today 26 September 1991). Their Director, David White, sided with the police against the team, even though the police were contravening Home Office policy on a number of counts. It took him nearly two years to modify his views (Beatrix Campbell, 1990).

In both these examples we see women being abused in an attempt to control them from speaking out as they seek to draw attention to the sexual abuse of children. We also see men in positions of authority denying the extent of the abuse. Thus Sigmund Freud, in his essay on 'Femininity' (1930) wrote 'almost all my women patients told me they had been seduced by their father'. Louise deSalvo says that he could not bring himself to believe that so many men in civilised Vienna were sexually abusing their daughters. 'Freud himself described that he abandoned the seduction theory' for this reason: 'there was the astonishing thing that in every case blame was laid on perverse acts by the father . . . it was hardly credible that perverted acts against children were so general'. (Louise deSalvo, 1991, quoting Marie Bonaparte, Anna Freud and Ernst Kris, 1954). So instead he decided that these women who had trusted him with their most painful secrets were fantasising. Louise deSalvo continues, 'However at the moment when Freud chose to deny the truth of his patients' experiences, he forfeited his ambition to understand the female neurosis.'

Freud's views have been enormously influential. Social workers and psychiatrists have not taken children's reports of abuse seriously, and little girls have been blaimed for being 'provocative'. Generations of psychiatrists, psychologists and social workers have also laid the blame for problems in the family on the mother. She is either 'smothering', or too distant and cold. If the father is abusive, she is to blame for colluding; if he is absent, she is to blame for not managing to keep him at home. 'She has been found guilty of being the schizophreno-genic mother . . . and [causing] anorexia nervosa' (Marilyn French, 1985), and producing 'latchkey children' by going out to work. We have a concept of 'fit mothering' but no one mentions 'fit fathering' (Jalna Hanmer and Daphne Statham, 1988). Many children are removed from mothers whose care is regarded as inadequate because they are thought to be unable to control an abusing father or cohabitee. It is only very recently that there have been demands to believe what children say and therefore face up to the extent of abuse.

Treatment of abusers

The most effective treatment of male abusers seems to be geared towards insisting that men face up to their responsibilities, acknowledge their behaviour and its effects, and stop blaming others. But it is a lengthy process for men to change attitudes that have been inculcated and learned since childhood. A man involved in this work writes:

> As I heard them talking about childhood and their early teen years, I was less and less able to deny how much we had in common. We grew up learning the same things about how to be men . . . We were taught that privilege is our birthright and aggression is our nature, so we learned to take but not to give. We learned to get affection, or express it, mainly through sex. We expected to marry a woman who would provide for us like a mother, but obey us like a daughter. And we learned that women and children belong to men, that there is nothing to keep us from using their labour for our benefit and their bodies for our pleasure and anger. (R. Snowdon, 1980)

Stephen Frosh, psychology lecturer at Birkbeck College and senior clinical psychologist at Lewisham child and family psychiatry clinic is quoted:

If there are systematic factors that make men more likely to abuse children sexually those factors will be present more or less strongly, in all men. This is perhaps one of the most crushing discoveries facing men who work with sexually abused children'. (Polly Neate, 1990)

Perhaps their managers should also pause for thought.
Another man writes:

> [workers] at the Men's Centre in London . . . do not believe that batterers are sick (there are far too many of them – unless we define masculinity as a sickness) . . . There is always an authority or control issue in the abusiveness. There is always challenge to his control prior to an abusive episode . . . We focus on how his violence and abusiveness are actually ways of asserting control . . . We are trying to teach him that the main issue in his relationships with women is his assumption of a right to be in charge and to expect servicing when, how and where he wants it. (Adam Jukes, 1990)

Masculinity

The accounts of these male writers suggest that abuse of power is strongly associated with masculinity as it is expressed in Western cultures at the present time. Martin Ruddock (1990), the team leader involved in the Kimberly Carlisle case, writes:

> I am concerned that many men in our society are in crisis. Men are predominantly the ones who abuse their power over others in ways which have led to the development of . . . child sexual abuse and domestic violence . . . I can't help but feel that we need to be paying more attention to masculinity . . . There are too many people for whom the frequent misuse of male power is too uncomfortable for us to ignore it any longer.

Gerry Popplestone (1987) describes how boys learn to become men:

> Everywhere a boy turns he is confronted by 'real men' images showing him what men are like, from Marlborough cowboys to self centred JR, on to men who drive Audi automatics. All of them know what to do: they win, every time . . . Boys learn to win through sports, through rough and tumble play, through competition . . . .

Phillip Hodson (1984) continues:

> By early teenage, boys are well into the important business of finding their place in the masculine pecking order. They are preoccupied with the deeds of their male contemporaries. They join that lifelong team or gang where there is always hope to impress. They fight, engage in contests . . . bully, cajole and browbeat their weaker brethren. Emotionally they learn the happy knack of making themselves feel better by making others feel worse . . . Boys are instructed from birth that you can only be somebody if you make external achievements which accredit you with power, financial or social. The corollary to this is that you cannot amount to anything in yourself, indeed you are not a person unless you have influence over some portion of the world at large. A man must be competitive with fellow males in order to achieve power . . . Men must manoeuvre openly to make their mark on the world . . . And the essence of masculine potency is that it robs another of status: I win, you lose.

Power and caring

Winning, achievement and mastery are at the heart of a man's identity. He gains these by exercising power and control over other people; over his own body (through sport and fitness training) and emotions; over his work (the breadwinner); and over other men, women, children, machines, technology and the environment with a 'compulsive concentration of energy on that which can be predicted, controlled, manipulated, possessed and preserved, piled up and counted' (Dorothy Dinnerstein, 1987). He expects women to continue what his mother did to support him in achieving his goals, bolster his masculine identity, and cater to his physical, emotional and sexual needs. In the family it is expected that this caring is offered for 'love': indeed, many women say that they returned to abusive partners because they loved them. If a man has no female relatives he pays other women for these services; for example cleaners and prostitutes. He also expects to be serviced at work by women receptionists, cleaners and secretaries.

We described in Chapter 2 how women learn to provide this caring for men, children and other dependents, and how it becomes part of their identity and means of fulfilment. Jean Baker Miller (1988), in her valuable book *Towards a New Psychology of Women*, describes how women's caring is often an attempt to interact with other people in ways that will foster the others' development and empower them to build up their strength, resources, effectiveness and well-being. Women's willingness to care and nurture reinforces men's expectations of being cared for, which in turn reinforces women in their caring role and enables men to retain their power. Thus men and women interact to support the separation of care and control.

We have seen in this book how this process is played out in the personal social services workplace: the caring and support tasks are delegated to women, who work in relatively low-paid, low-status jobs; management emphasises control functions, and tends to be monopolised by white men.

What is missing in this interaction is a recognition by women and men that *everyone*, including women, needs to be cared for in order to realise their potential, and that the ethic and act of caring is fundamental not just to being a *woman*, but also to being a *human being*. This missing link is responsible for the abusive situations to which we have repeatedly referred. Not only do men abuse women, but women unintentionally abuse themselves by accepting without question that it is their role to do all the caring.

In caring for others, most women pay insufficient attention to their own needs for support, development and fulfilment, except in so far as this is achieved through caring for others. We see numerous examples of women sacrificing themselves for others to the detriment of their own health, well-being and development of themselves as people because they are unable to set limits on what is demanded of them, sometimes do not appreciate that they themselves have needs, and often do not regard themselves as worthy of care. This has come about, as we have explained, through being taught for hundreds of years that it is their duty to care for others. Initial attempts by individual women to change their situation often meet with accusations of selfishness because those cared for do not wish to lose out. This can easily lead to guilt and anxiety in the carer.

We have suggested that the public face of the personal social services gives a false impression by emphasising caring and playing down the necessary control functions. Good caring requires control of the people being cared for by setting necessary limits on their behaviour and encouraging them to retain as much independence as possible. Limits also need to be put on the caring in order to maintain its quality and protect the carer. This provides space for her own needs to be met in ways which do not involve caring for others. In other words, the rights of both the carer and the cared for must be respected.

Most women who succeed in exercising their power to control other people's demands on them find the process itself empowering because it enables them to develop other talents, increase their self respect, and gain more control over their lives.

Setting suitable limits is a delicate process as the control exercised slips into abuse if it becomes excessive. Those in powerful positions need to retain or develop a strong caring strand to temper the control that they exercise. Power is less likely to be abused by those who have learned to care for others because caring involves empathising with others in order to meet their needs.

It is evident that the caring strand of management has been seriously neglected. Rehabilitating it would not only help to prevent abuse, it would also break down the barriers between managers and people in caring jobs. It would lessen the culture clash caused by two sets of values which often seem to be opposed. A more caring management would be more appreciative of women managers' contributions, and could learn much from their approach. Appointing more women managers and valuing what they bring to management would be one way of achieving such changes. A more caring culture would in itself attract more women into management, and if their contributions were valued they would become more confident in exercising their power.

Working for change

In the past, women were thought to be 'naturally' good at caring, but incapable of 'more responsible' jobs; men were considered to have a divine right to be in charge, and to be useless at washing up or changing nappies.

Many women have challenged these notions, and the movement for change is growing. Substantial numbers of women are no longer prepared to confine their means of fulfilment to caring for others. They wish to decide for themselves what sort of life to lead and be respected as individuals whatever kind of work they are doing, whether paid work in a job or unpaid work in the home. At the same time, many of them are reluctant to adopt the attitudes and life style of working men, which they see as sacrificing many of the more humane values associated with caring. A few men have joined these women in challenging previous assumptions about what men and women should be and do. They are discovering new satisfactions in involving themselves in bringing up children and other caring and support activities previously defined as 'women's work', and are prepared to support women in their struggle for recognition and respect in other activities.

All women and men in Western societies have been influenced by these changes, which are reflected in changed expectations and ways of life. However, most men recognise that they have a lot to lose by relinquishing control, and do not realise that there are many advantages. The movement amongst men for change is still in its infancy.

10

Strategies

In this chapter we will be looking at some ways in which women managers in the personal social services and those women who may become managers can develop strategies to alter their situations so that they can do their jobs more effectively, and obtain more satisfaction from them. We will also look at what can be done by organisations (and the people who currently manage them) and by society at large to encourage more women into management posts.

Organisational strategies

Equal opportunities policies

Equal opportunities policies are part of good management and vital in every organisation to promote equality for women; black, older and disabled people; and gay men and lesbians. Such policies can be a powerful reference point for individual or collective action. They enable women and other groups to challenge discrimination more effectively.

● Equal opportunities policies need to be worked out in detail and backed by disciplinary procedures.
● Policies should be clear, written down, and generally accessible. Training must be provided for all staff to brief them on the implementation of the policies.
● Senior managers must be committed to equal opportunities in order for policies to be effective: 'Managers need to equip themselves with an understanding of the processes

140

which unfairly disadvantage women at work, and must be committed to tackling them. For male managers this means challenging and changing some of the processes which have helped them to succeed' (Denise Platt, 1991).

● Many organisations do already have equal opportunities policies but there is a need for further development and refinement. Creative thinking is necessary to promote positive action. The targeting being introduced by some authorities (see Chapter 6) is a promising development. Targeting is a means of measuring standards of performance of equal opportunities policies, to allow for necessary corrective action. They are not quotas (*Equal Opportunities Review* March/April 1990).

● Services offered should be sensitive to, and reflect the needs of, the consumers. (If a particular group of people is not making use of the services, there should be consultation with their representatives.) Making services relevant does not necessarily mean increased costs.

● Managers can be influential in ensuring effective and sensitive implementation of equal opportunities policies in their part of the organisation. They can also influence the initiation and development of policies, for example by drawing attention to discrimination against staff and consumers. Julia Ross (1990) suggests that the hiring policies of local authorities could include packages of child care facilities for staff, encouraging the predominant culture to shift away from the idea that men should be in charge. She continues, 'Men should note that unless the attitudes and behaviour of people in the organisation are sympathetic [to women] then change is unlikely to occur'.

● Work must continue in encouraging women to participate on a genuinely equal basis to men by ensuring that more technical, scientific and managerial posts are really open to all equally. Selection to such posts should be based on skills and knowledge to do the job well, rather than on a narrow definition of what the job entails, which is often based on 'masculine' attributes. Job descriptions must be 'rigorously reviewed' to see if they contain any gender assumptions about the nature of the work (Denise Platt, 1991).

Organisational structure and culture

If the entrenched sexist attitudes of most organisations are to change then people have to know the structure and culture of the organisation in which they work in order to play their part in initiating, encouraging and carrying through such changes. Having a wide knowledge of the people, structures and systems of the organisation, the 'folkways for action' (John Stewart and Michael Clarke, 1990) enables women to understand the processes operating and where the power is based and thus be powerful themselves.

● It is important to know and understand the policies of the organisation so that those leading to or underpinning sexist behaviour can be altered, and those encouraging and supporting staff to a gender sensitive approach in their work can be encouraged and fostered. Organisational culture affects attitudes to women in an organisation but is also itself affected by individuals.

● One London Social Services Department involved women employees in a consultation exercise which produced suggestions for changing the agency culture. These included developing a culture that views the whole person, recognising the experience of women, implementing women's development courses, and having clearer expectations of women's roles (London Borough of Hammersmith and Fulham, 1986).

● Women can resist automatically doing the caring and servicing jobs.

● Language, both verbal and written, should be gender sensitive.

● Any sexual harassment needs to be stopped by prompt action as soon as it is identified. It should be treated as a disciplinary matter. Offensive or potentially offensive material should be destroyed (Michael Rubenstein, 1991). Positive images of women and other under-represented groups should be encouraged.

Training

Training is important for everyone to do their job effectively. For women, training often gives confidence as well as appropriate knowledge and skills with which to do the job better. Because women have different management training needs from men, there is a need for both single and mixed gender training. Women-only training needs are likely to include preparation for management, women in management, personal and career development and re-entry training.

● Training must be recognised as an essential part of any and every job.
● Release from and cover for work duties when staff are training should be an automatic right.
● Women can ensure that they take up training opportunities on offer in and through their agencies.
● Stringent efforts should be made to enable everyone to have access to training. Access to training should be monitored.
● Training being offered should be appropriate for women and where both women and men are involved together on courses, men should not be allowed to take over. This can be achieved by ensuring that women are not in the minority on particular courses, that women trainers are used, and that images and examples validate women. In the same way, training should enable all groups to be included and validated.
● Social work training should include management training, reflecting the fact that management is a part of everyone's job and encouraging women to transfer the skills which they already possess.

Management practice and style

Management practice and style has a profound effect on the culture of an organisation and vice versa. At present the way management is practised and management styles are based on traditional views about what management is and what kinds of people are managers. We would like to see women managers influencing this situation so that a new understanding of management is developed. In this way new styles of management can evolve for both women and men.

● Women managers should challenge rather than 'fit into' existing models of managing. These are often particularly inappropriate in the personal social services, which aims to provide a caring service for consumers. Veronica Coulshed (1990[1]), writing about social work management, says that if women behave 'like men in a man's world', they pay the price of physical and emotional illness that such styles of management can lead to. She continues, 'One of the problems is that there is a paucity of literature in social work management which focuses on other perspectives (for instance ethnic and feminist research and orientations towards leadership roles). Thus we have borrowed ideas rather than challenge this male management behaviour'.

● Both men and women managers can bring a more 'holistic' style to their work by validating the caring side of managing in the personal social services and insisting on recognising that people have domestic and personal as well as work commitments.

● Men's lifestyles and ways of behaving do not have to be considered as the norm. Women should not have to act like men to be taken seriously.

● Managers can develop an assertive rather than an aggressive style of communicating with others. When communicating, people can stand up for themselves, ensure that they are heard, listen properly to others and speak out for what they know is right. It is not necessary to communicate in an aggressive controlling way which either diminishes others or allows individuals to be diminished by being too passive.

● People can manage in a co-operative, supportive way that empowers others, and enlists their support, attaining consensus rather than in a way which encourages people to rate others in a hierarchical structure.

- People can manage in a flexible style which allows creativity and can incorporate individuals working in ways which encourage them to develop their own style of working rather than forcing people to fit into a 'hidebound' system that does not suit anyone but maintains rules from which no one really benefits.

Use of power in the organisation

Power can be used in a caring way to empower other people, both colleagues and consumers, to do and achieve things. Power can also be used to control and achieve things at the expense of other people.

If shared, power is far less open to abuse than if it is concentrated in the hands of too few people. Also, if shared, this need not diminish either the status or the decision-making role of any one person.

- People can pay more attention to the way in which they use power in their work. They can develop 'empowering' skills and limit their use of 'controlling power'.
- Women can reconceptualise their understanding of power and so learn to be less afraid of using the power invested in their work position and role. They can take hold of their power and use it more directly.
- Management as empowerment can also mean sharing power with others. This creates a culture of work that enables everyone to work well, encourages the development of others, values everyone's contribution and enables everyone to contribute to the full extent of their abilities. Such a culture is much more in tune with the caring values generally promoted by the personal social services, but not often practised by managers.
- Managers who are prepared to use power in positive ways can do much to further initiatives in implementing equal opportunities policies whether or not these exist within their own sphere of work. Most teams are quite autonomous (one advantage of not being closely supervised) so it is usually possible to 'take power in one's own hands'.

Meg Bond (1989) describes how she helped to empower a group of women staff in a home for elderly people to take control of the weekly staffing rota in a way that promoted the interests of both the staff and the residents:

> More often than not the rota is seen by staff as handed down from above, as an expression of management control. In an attempt to challenge this traditional male management approach of imposition we discussed the difficulties of the rota. Importantly and unusually we took account of people's feelings and outside commitments . . . We decided that the rota should:
>
> - promote continuity of care for residents . . .
> - promote teamwork among staff . . .
> - preserve minimum standards of cover . . .
> - respect staff contracts in terms of hours and rates of pay . . .
> - take account of the domestic commitments of staff . . .
>
> We thus recognised our common interests as front line staff and seniors, as waged and unwaged carers, and developed a set of guidelines to promote our shared and individual well being.

This example shows that power does not have to be used to assert dominance and control over others. It can be used to empower others, so attaining equality and respect between people. This then improves both working conditions for staff and the services which they provide for consumers.

● Men must develop an understanding of how their desire to dominate and control others has been institutionalised. They must learn to share their power and to empower others.
● Decision-making should be shared as widely as possible to include all levels of staff, and consumers wherever appropriate. This creates a culture of work that enables everyone to contribute to the full extent of their abilities, values everyone's contribution equally, encourages people's development and so creates a culture of work enabling everyone to work well.

Personal and social strategies

Caring for oneself and others

There has been much discussion throughout this book about the assumption that caring is 'women's work' and not for men to do. This imbalance needs to be corrected. Women could then have more freedom to develop their careers and men could develop their home-making and parenting skills. Cary Cooper and Valerie Sutherland (1991) have done research showing that men are now less willing 'to accept the workaholic success-at-any-price ideology'.

● Caring itself needs to be reclaimed as a valuable activity with which everybody should be involved. Veronica Coulshed (1990[2]) describes caring as sensitive maintenance and support work which should be given high priority. It should no longer be seen as low status work done by women. It is a part of normal human activity and a skill to be learnt and practised like any other by both men and women. Men must learn that caring does not detract from their masculinity.
● Men should not be cared for either at home or at work (meals cooked and appointments made for them) just because they are men.
● Women can learn to care for themselves better than they tend to do at present. This includes sharing the caring tasks with men, and encouraging others to care for them when appropriate.

Marianne Skelcher (1987) says that women need to find ways of doing jobs and managing pressures that meet their needs as women and without blaming themselves for getting into the trap of having no emotional or physical resources left.

● Women can protect themselves from the effects of excessive stress by caring for themselves outside work, eating well and taking exercise, as well as having enjoyable leisure time where they do not continue to do any caring.

● Men can ensure that caring work is not merely relegated to their women colleagues at work and partners at home. Women can also ensure that they do not take on the caring role inappropriately by seeing themselves just as carers, but acknowledging their skills and potential for development in all areas of life and work. They can resist automatically doing the caring and servicing jobs.

● Women can be clear at work and in their personal lives about roles and boundaries. Debbie Clarke (1987) talks about jobs being so big that hardly anyone, especially women, would want to do them. She suggests that jobs can be humanised and cut down so that they are more targeted and realistic. If men were properly involved in caring work in the home, they would not be prepared to tolerate the '80 hour week'. An effective challenge to this could also open up more management posts to women.

Julia Phillipson (1990) has a list of very positive suggestions for women when they are at work. This includes not underestimating what one knows one can do; being kind to oneself; celebrating achievements; and learning from mistakes.

● Personal social service agencies can offer relevant sensitive caring for consumers. This means that services should be such as to empower consumers, rather than patronise them or make them feel inadequate and failures because they are in need of such services.

● Staff welfare is important. Jeff Hopkins (1991) says, 'Staff care is seen as a proactive service. It addresses issues of personal distress and low morale, staff absence and staff retention.' He points out that there is considerable disruption and insecurity in the personal social services which gives rise to concern about the general state of well-being within the profession. He emphasises that staff care is not a panacea for the problems of inadequate resourcing. However, staff welfare can affect the culture of the workplace and so is a resource for bringing about positive changes in the position, role and status of women at work.

● Caring responsibilities should not be disadvantageous to women in terms of recognition of their skills for the job and prospects of promotion (SSI, 1991).

Networking

Since men have their own networks, it is important that women too create networks for themselves. This can be done by actively seeking out kindred spirits or valuable contacts. Some women take a note of names, addresses and telephone numbers of any women they meet who could conceivably be a useful contact in the future. These contacts can be both in and outside the work organisation. Networking can provide support, strength, information and friendship. Having a mentor is part of networking. A mentor is someone who has usually attained success in her chosen field and can now encourage, advise and support others who follow suit, as well as acting as a role model. Networking is vital for women and black managers as they are usually isolated in white-male-dominated environments.

Networking with other women in their own and other organisations and from personal contacts can help women to deal with sexism and to get encouragement for developing their careers and potential. It can encourage women to do things that are a challenge as well as providing support. Jean Woollard and Miranda Lowe (1988) call this 'tough love'. They say, 'We offered a shoulder to cry on when it was needed but we also encouraged each other to do things which would challenge us and build our confidence'. They describe how so many women are conditioned to believe that in some way they are not good enough, and that this is so ingrained as to feel 'normal'. The task is for these self-destructive patterns of behaviour to be contradicted so that women can allow themselves to think and act with their full potential. In other words, women can empower themselves and each other to plan and act on positive changes they want for themselves in the context of self- and mutual validation.

Some women choose to network only with other women, but as David Clutterbuck (1990) points out, this can exclude them from the power bases (usually predominantly male-dominated) with which they are trying to effect change. Black women may choose to network with black men because of their common experience of racism.

- Through networking women can ensure that they get appropriate support for themselves and they can offer support to other women.
- They can actively set up network structures and support groups for themselves and others.
- They can find a mentor for themselves and then be available to help other women who are less advanced in their careers.
- Networking should be acknowledged by management as an appropriate part of work. Time and opportunity should be given for this during work hours.

Examples of networks in existence at the time writing are:

a network of black women in senior posts in both the public and private sectors in London;

a women's management 'working group' convened by the Local Government Management Board;

an association of women managers in the personal social services based in the North of England;

a group of women in social work education who meet regularly in London;

a network of women managers working in local government;

a European Women's Management Development Network.

Career planning and training

Unlike men, women are not accustomed to planning their lives. Very often they remain in jobs with no prospect of promotion because they have never given much thought to their future.

- Women just as much as men can give their paid work more serious attention rather than as just a job to earn money.

● Women can make conscious choices about which jobs they apply for and at what stage of their careers and lives. It is important that women do not let themselves 'drift' in their work but make definite, clear decisions about their careers.

● They can be assertive about their ambitions, identifying learning opportunities they want to seize and making the most of them (David Clutterbuck, 1990).

● It is important for women not to miss out on or to avoid prospects of promotion just because they have domestic responsibilities or feel that their career is not as vital as that of a partner.

● Girls at school can ensure that they obtain a good general education and not dismiss this because they are planning to marry and have a family. Women at work can ensure that they make the best use of those training opportunities which are available and appropriate to their domestic and work situations.

● Women can take risks in terms of going for jobs or training that they know they can do but about which they feel diffident.

● Social work training should re-examine the way in which students are taught to handle emotions. An emotional content is expected in caring. Yet social work trains people to distance themselves from clients. Part of any social work training course is concerned with teaching students to control their emotions. At the same time, in a contradictory way, qualities such as emotional warmth are encouraged. At the management level, however, emotions are again considered to be inappropriate. Women managers are often criticised for being 'too emotional'. It is significant that such comments invariably come from men. Most women have mixed feelings when they are criticised by men for being too emotional. On the one hand this means they are not taken seriously, and on the other hand they do not want to lose touch with the caring aspects of social work. They face the dilemma of distancing themselves from the situations of both the people they are managing and the consumers, or of being considered (by their male colleagues) of being over-involved and feeling responsible for them. Even though men tend to have difficulties in expressing their emotions and they are not taught to care for others as part of their upbringing, they undergo the same social work training as women, being taught that emotions need to be controlled. When they become managers they find it difficult to engage with the painful aspects of the work, usually avoiding the caring side of management, and regarding emotions as inappropriate even to working in the personal social services. Social work educators must recognize that there is a need for gender-specific training to take account of these different needs.

Social policy and legislation

In Britain there is confusion as to whether the government wants women to stay at home to care for dependents or whether they should be encouraged into employment with provision for child care and supporting responsibilities.

In Sweden, the government has taken a strategic role, developing a policy framework for equal opportunities in the workplace based on four components. Firstly, there is a substantial period of paid 'parental leave' (eighteen months). Secondly, either parent has the right to work part-time until a child is eight years old. Thirdly, parents have the right to up to ninety days per child per year paid leave if the child is sick. Fourthly, there are sufficient public-funded child care facilities both for pre-school age children, and out-of-school care for children of school age. Underpinning this policy are principles that child care should be publicly funded, that it should be community-based and not provided by employers, that men too are responsible for children, and that a balance needs to be struck between paid work, family life and other activities (Jane Brotchie, 1990).

● There needs to be universal, adequate maternity benefit and leave, also sufficient respite care and home services for dependant adults (Maggie Meade-King, 1990). This should be provided by public funds rather than left to employers, so that there is national parity and government control over such provisions. Celia Weston (1990) quotes Joanna Foster, chairperson of the Equal Opportunities Commission, as saying 'The nature and size of the challenge [of women bridging the skills gap] makes this much too big and complex an issue to be left to market forces. Employers cannot afford this by themselves. The government must help.'

● Equal opportunities laws must be strengthened. An example of firmer legislation is the Northern Ireland Fair Employment Act, 1990. This Act specifies that employers have to monitor their labour force. The penalties for not adhering to this legislation are fines of up to £30,000 and the withdrawal of government contracts.

Conclusion

As we were writing this chapter, 'Opportunity 2000' was being launched. This initiative, designed to boost the representation of women at all levels of work, was backed by leading firms in the private sector, as well as by the National Health Service. Certain local authorities had previously led the field in promoting equal opportunites. Unless they too join or match this initiative, they are in danger of being overtaken by the private sector.

However, the personal social services still has a trump card. It still pays lip-service to a culture of caring, and the vast majority of its grass-roots staff are committed to retaining caring as a primary strand of their work. Many women managers are endeavouring to support this caring ethic and are challenging the controlling culture of management.

We have argued that the way management is practised has become distorted. It is seen by the men who occupy most of the jobs, write books on the subject and tutor management courses as essentially a controlling activity. Consequently the important caring strand is neglected. The relatively few women in management posts tend to have different priorities and a different view of management, giving due place to its essential caring activities. Some of the more recent management theories also emphasise the importance of good human relationship skills and attention to quality of service. We would like to see women represented in management in a similar proportion to their representation in other jobs in the personal social services. We believe that if even 50 per cent of managers were women, they would have a profound effect on the culture of their organisations.

Here is an opportunity readily available to improve both the quality of services offered and the nature of working life in the personal social services. In turn, it could act as an exciting model for other organisations.

Appendix

In this section we list a selection of books and organisations, some of which we have mentioned in the text, which may be useful to readers of this book.

Equal Opportunities Commission
Overseas House
Quay Street
Manchester   M3 3HN
Tel: 061 833 9244

Helpful information department about all aspects of equality for women and work.

Equal Opportunities Commission
St Andrews House
141 West Nile Street
Glasgow   G1 2RN
Tel: 041 332 8018

EOC (Welsh Regional Office)
Caerwys House
Windsor Lane
Cardiff   CF1 1LB
Tel: 0222 343 552

EOC for Northern Ireland
Chamber of Commerce House
22,Great Victoria Street
Belfast   BT2 2BA
Tel: 0232 242752

Sexual harassment

Women Against Sexual Harassment (WASH)
242 Pentonville Road
London   N1 9UN

Sexual Harassment of Women in the Workplace:
A Guide to Legal Action
Available from WASH (address above).

Job sharing

Job Sharing, a Practical Guide
Pam Walton (Kogan Page, 1990).

New Ways to Work
309 Upper Street
London   N1 2TY
Tel: 071 226 4026

(Job sharing information)

Careers – courses, books and papers

Moving into Management – a course for women
Obtainable from:
Customer Services Department
The Open College
Freepost
St James Buildings
Oxford Road
Manchester   M1 6DR

(At the time of writing, the cost of this pack was £80.)

Women into Management
Details from:
Open Business School
The Open University
Walton Hall
Milton Keynes
Bucks   MK7 6AA

The Springboard Workbook,
Hawthorne Press
Bankfield House
13 Wallbridge
Stroud
Glos   Gl5 3JR

Working Choices – A life planning guide for women today
Jane Skinner and Rennie Fritchie (Dent, 1988)

What Colour is Your Parachute?
Richard Bolles
Ten Speed Press, 1981

What else can a secretary do?
Available from:
COIC Sales Department
Freepost
Sheffield   S1 4BR

Women's Link.
A news letter for women in the social services.
Available from:
The Local Government Management Board
Arndale House
Arndale Centre
Luton
Beds   LU1 2TS

Careers – organisations

Central Council for Training and Education in Social Work
Derbyshire House
St Chad's Street
London   WC1H 8AD
Tel: 071 278 2455

National Council for Vocational Qualifications
222 Euston Road
London   NW1 2BZ
Tel: 071 387 9898

Careers Offices. For local address, check phone book

Career Analysts
Career House
90 Gloucester Place
London   W1H 4BL
Tel: 071 935 5452

Careers for Women
Fourth floor
2 Valentine Place
London   SE1 8QH

Impact
PO Box 905
Marlow
Bucks   SL7 2UA
Tel: 0628 898 083

Independent Assessment and Research Centre
17 Portland Place
London   W1N 3AF
Tel: 071 935 2372

National Advisory Centre on Careers for Women (NACCW)
30 Gordon Street
London   W1H OAX
Tel: 071 380 0117

National Education Guidance Initiative
Bowling Green Terrace
Leeds   LS11 9SX

The Pepperell Unit
The Industrial Society
Robert Hyde House
48, Bryanston Square
London   W1H 7LN
Tel: 071 935 2600

Women and Training Group GLOSCAT
Oxstalls Lane
Glos   GL2 9HW
Tel: 0452 426836/7/8

Educational Guidance Service for Adults
Room 208
Bryson House,
28, Bedford Street
Belfast   BT2 7FE
Tel: 0232 244 274

References

ABC News (1970) *The Eye of the Storm* (video available from Concord Films, Ipswich.

Abdela, L. (1991) 'It is like waiting for fish to grow feet', *Independent*, 25 September.

Ahmad, B. (1990) *Black Perspectives in Social Work*, Birmingham, Venture Press.

Bailey, R. and M. Break (eds) (1977) *Radical Social Work*, London, Edward Arnold.

Baker Miller, J. (1988) *Toward a New Psychology of Women*, Harmondsworth, Penguin.

Baker Miller, J. (1982) *Women and Power*, Stone Center Working Paper Series, Wellesley College, Mass.

Barr, H. (1987) *Perspectives on Training for Residential Work*, London, CCETSW.

Baxandall, R., E. Ewen and L. Gordon (1976) 'The working class has two sexes', *Monthly Review*, July–August.

Beagley, J. (1986) 'Why men manage and women are the workforce', *Community Care Supplement*, 18 September.

Beechey, V. and T. Perkins (1987) *A Matter of Hours: Women, Part Time Work and the Labour Market*, Cambridge, Polity Press.

Benet, M. (1972) *Secretary*, London, Sidgwick & Jackson.

Bolger, S., P. Corrigan, J. Docking and N. Frost (1981) *Towards Socialist Welfare Work*, London, Macmillan.

Bonaparte, M., A. Freud and E. Kris (eds) (1954) *Origins of Psychoanalysis: Letters to Wilhelm Fleiss*, London, Imago.

Bond, M. (1989) 'Management in the homes', *Community Care*, 9 March.

Bone, A. (1983) *Girls and Girls Only Schools: A Review of the Evidence*, Manchester, EOC.

Booth, T. (1987) 'Camden shows the way', *Community Care*, 26 February.

159

Booth, T. (1990) 'Taking the plunge', *Community Care*, 26 July.

Bowlby, J. (1967) *Child Care and the Growth of Love*, Harmondsworth, Penguin.

Brook, E and A. Davis (1985) *Women, the Family, and Social Work*, London, Tavistock.

Brotchie, J. (1990) 'First the good news', *Community Care*, 20 November.

Brown, C. (1984) *Black and White Britain*, London, Policy Studies Institute.

Burden, D. and N. Gottlieb (eds) (1987) *The Woman Client: Providing Human Services in a Changing World*, London, Tavistock.

Butler, L. (1991) 'Accrediting women's unpaid work and experience', *Adult Learning*, vol. 2, no. 7, March.

Caines , E. (1991) Address to National Association of Health Authorities and Trusts Annual Conference, Bournemouth, September.

Camden, London Borough of (1987) *Independent Review of Residential Care for the Elderly*, February.

Cameron, D. (1990) 'An ideology for the job', *Community Care*, 17 May.

Campbell, B. (1988) *Unofficial Secrets*, London, Virago.

Campbell, B. (1990) 'Children's stories', *New Statesman and Society*, 5 October.

CCETSW (1992) *Finance for Students Resident in England and Wales Taking Dip. SW Programmes or CQSW Courses*, Information sheet 15; Information Sheet 15s for students resident in Scotland; Information sheet 17 for students resident in Northern Ireland (January).

Clarke, D. (1987) 'Working with Men', in J. Underwood (ed.)., *Asserting the Female Perspective*, Working paper 69, University of Bristol School for Advanced Urban Studies.

Clutterbuck, D. (1990) 'Building bridges to top management', *Women and Training News*, April.

Cockburn, C. (1987) *Women, Trade Unions and Political Parties*, Fabian Research Series 349, London, The Fabian Society, September.

Cockburn, C. (1988) 'The Gendering of Jobs: Workplace Relations and the Reproduction of Sex Segregation', in S. Walby (ed.), *Gender Segregation at Work*, Milton Keynes, Open University Press.

Community Care (1989) 'Roman soldier in AD66', *Community Care*, 6 July.

Cooper, C. (1991) 'Whose fault is it anyway?', BBC Radio 4, 2 May.

Cooper, C. and V. Sutherland (1991) 'Transfers put staff under stress', *Guardian*, 15 April.

Coote, A. and B. Campbell (1987) *Sweet Freedom*, Oxford, Basil Blackwell.

Coote, A. and P. Pattullo (1990) *Power and Prejudice: Women and Politics*, London, Weidenfeld & Nicolson.

Corrigan, P. and P. Leonard (1979) *Social Work Practice under Capitalism: A Marxist Approach*, London, Macmillan.

Coulshed,. V. (1990[1]) *Management in Social Work*, London, Macmillan.

Coulshed, V. (1990[2]) 'Soapbox', *Social Work Today*, 11 October.

Court of Appeal (1991) Ruling on rape in marriage, March.

Coward, R. (1990) 'Introducing the family', *Guardian*, 14 August

Coyle, A. (1989) 'The limits of change: local government and equal opportunities for women', *Public Administration*, 67.

Coyle, A. and J. Skinner (1988) *Women and Work: Positive Action for Change*, London, Macmillan.

Cuthbert, N. (1970) *Management Thinkers*, Harmondsworth, Penguin.

Daily Telegraph (1991) 23 January.

Dale, J. and P. Foster (1986) *Feminists and State Welfare*, London, Routledge & Kegan Paul.

Dalley, G. (1988) *Ideologies of Caring: Rethinking Community and Collectivism*, London, Macmillan.

Davidson, M. and C. Cooper (1983) *Stress and the Woman Manager*, Oxford, Robertson.

Davis, L. (1982) *Residential Care: A Community Resource*, London, William Heinemann.

Dawson, J. (1990) 'Vortex of evil', *New Statesman and Society*, 5 October.

DeSalvo, L. (1991) *Virginia Woolf: The Impact of Childhood Sexual Abuse on Her Life and Work*, London, The Women's Press.

DHSS (Department of Health and Social Security) (1976) *Personal Social Services*, Local Authority Statistics, ref. S/F77/3.

DHSS (Department of Health and Social Security) (1986) *Decisions in Child Care*, HMSO.

Dickens, C. (1986) *David Copperfield*, Harmondsworth, Penguin.

Dinnage, R. (1989) Unpublished M. Phil. thesis, Brunel University, Uxbridge.

Dinnerstein, D. (1987) *The Rocking of the Cradle and the Ruling of the World*, London, Women's Press.

Durran, J. (1989) 'Continuous agitation', *Community Care*, 13 July.

Eley, R. (1986) 'An examination of the role of the senior social worker analyzed from a gender perspective', unpublished MA dissertation, Liverpool University.

Eley, R. (1989) 'Women in Management in Social Services Departments', in C. Hallett (ed.), *Women and Social Services Departments*, Brighton, Harvester Wheatsheaf.

Eliot, G. (1974) *The Mill on the Floss*, London, J. M.Dent.

Equal Opportunities Commission (1991) *Women and Men in Britain*, EOC.

Equal Opportunities Review (1990[1]) 'Employing people with disabilities: the Birmingham approach', *Equal Opportunites Review*, no. 29, January/February.

Equal Opportunities Review (1990[2]) 'Positive action in the West Midlands', no. 30, March/April.

Equal Opportunities Review (1990[3]) no. 33, September/October.

Equal Opportunities Review (1990[4]) no. 34, November/December.

European Commission (1991) *Child Care in the European Community 1985–1990*, Brussels.

Fant, O. with A. Cohen, M. Cox and R. Kanter (1980) 'A Tale of "O": On Being Different, A Training Tool for Managing Diversity', Good Measure Inc., Cambridge, Mass. Distributed by Melrose Film Productions, London.

Finch, J. and D. Groves (eds) (1983) *A Labour of Love: Women, Work and Caring*, London, Routledge & Kegan Paul.

Forster, M. (1986) *Significant Sisters: The Grassroots of Active Feminism 1839–1939*, Harmondsworth, Penguin.

Foster, J. (1987) 'Women on the wane', *Insight*, 14 December.

Foster, J. (1988[1]) 'On the hop', *Insight*, 27 May.

Foster, J. (1988[2]) 'Girls on top', *Insight*, 3 June.

Foster, J. (1990) 'Women's careers; challenge, choices and constraints', unpublished paper presented at BASW Conference, 'Women of the 90s'.

Frankl, G. (1989) *The Social History of the Unconscious*, London, Open Gate Press.

French, M. (1985) *Beyond Power: On Women, Men and Morals*, London and Harmondsworth, Abacus.

Freud, S. (1974) *Introductory Lectures on Psychoanalysis* (1917) Pelican Freud Library 1, Harmondsworth, Penguin.

Freud, S. (1977) *Some Psychical Consequences of the Anatomical Distinction between the Sexes* (1925) Pelican Freud Library 7, Harmondsworth, Penguin.

Freud, S. (1981) *Female Sexuality* (1930), Complete works 21, London, Hogarth Press.

Freud, S. (1954/1985) *Origins of Psychoanalysis: Letters to Wilhelm Fleiss*, in M. Bonaparte *et al.* (eds), London, Imago 1954 and J. Mason (ed.), Cambridge, Mass., Harvard University Press, 1985.

Fry, A. (1991) 'Women at the top', *Social Work Today*, 16 May.

Glaser, D. and S. Frosh (1988) *Child Sexual Abuse*, London, Macmillan.

Gledhill, N. (1989) 'Only people with disabilities need apply', *Equal Opportunities Review*, no.23, January/February.

Golding, V. (1988) 'In the firing line', *Insight*, 4 March.

Griffiths, R. (1988) *Community Care: An Agenda for Action*, London, HMSO.

Grigg, A. (1989) 'Boys a brain drain', *The Times*, 4 September.

Guardian (1990[1]) Report 27 July.

Guardian (1990[2]) Report 14 August.

Guardian (1991) 'Working for childcare', 16 April.

Hammersmith and Fulham, London Borough of (1986) Women's Consultation Exercise in the Social Services, 4 December.

Hallett, C. (ed.) (1989) *Women and Social Services Departments*, Brighton, Harvester Wheatsheaf.

Handy, C. (1986) *Understanding Organisations*, Harmondsworth, Penguin.

Hanmer, J. and D. Statham (1988) *Women and Social Work: Towards a Woman-Centred Practice*, London, Macmillan.

Hilsum, S. and K. Start (1974) *Promotion and Careers in Teaching*, National Foundation for Educational Research, Slough.

Hirsch, W. and S. Bevan (1988) *What Makes a Manager?*, Falmer, Sussex, Institute of Manpower Studies.

HMSO (1946) *Report of the Committee on the Care of Children*, Cmnd 6922, London, HMSO.

HMSO (1970) *Local Authorities Social Services Act 1970*, London, HMSO.

HMSO (1974) *Local Government Act 1974*, London, HMSO.

HMSO (1975) *Sex Discrimination Act 1975*, London, HMSO.

HMSO (1989) *Caring for People: Community Care in the Next Decade and Beyond*, London, HMSO.

HM Treasury (1986) *Using Private Enterprise in Government*, London, HMSO.

Hodson, P. (1984) *Men, an Investigation into the Emotional Male*, London, Ariel Books, BBC.

Hollinger, P. (1991) 'Grooming girls for the career ladder', *Financial Times*, 3 February.

Hopkins, J. (1991) 'Caring for staff must come first', *Community Care* (Inside) 31 January.

Horrell, S. and J. Rubery (1991) *Employers' Working Time Policies and Women's Employment*, London, HMSO.

House of Lords (1991) *Regina* v. *R.*, 23 October.

Howe, D. (1986) 'The segregation of women and their work in the personal social services', *Critical Social Policy*, no. 15, Spring.

Hughes, J. (1988) 'The body of knowledge in management education', *Journal of Management Education and Development*, vol. 19, no. 4.

Hull, C. (1990) 'Making the most of career breaks', *Adults Learning*, vol. 2, no. 4, December.

International Labour Organisation (1980) Study presented at the women's conference in Copenhagen

Jacklyn, C. (1991) *Sex, Differentiation and Schooling*, London, Heinemann.

Jeffreys, S. (1985) *The Spinster and her Enemies: Feminism and Sexuality 1880–1930*, London, Pandora.

Jongeward, D. and D. Scott (eds) (1975) *Affirmative Action for Women: A Practical Guide for Women and Management*, Reading, Mass., Addison-Wesley.

N. Josefowitz (1986) *Paths to Power*, Bromley, Kent, Columbus Books.

Jukes, A. (1990) 'Making women safe', *Social Work Today*, 21 June.

Kanter, R. (1977) *Men and Women of the Corporation*, New York, Basic Books.

Kanter, R. (1984) *Change Masters: Corporate Entrepreneurs at Work*, London, George Allen & Unwin.

Katz, I. and D. Brindle (1991) 'Avuncular figure who stole childhoods. Four questions on the duty of care', *Guardian*, 30 November.

Kilbrandon, L. (1964) Child & Young Persons Scotland, Report by the Committee appointed by the Secretary of State for Scotland, Cmnd 2306, Edinburgh, HMSO.

Lancelot, M. (1990[1]) 'Women in social service departments: not at the peaks', *Community Care*, 28 June.

Lancelot, M. (1990[2]) 'A fitting model for the 90s', *Community Care*, 5 July.

Langrish, S. (1981) 'Why don't women progress to management jobs?', *Business Graduate*, no. 11.

Levy, A. (1991) *The Social Services Inspectorate Report into Child Protection in Staffordshire 1990*, London, HMSO.

Loden, M. (1985) *Feminine Leadership. How to Succeed in Business without Being One of the Boys*, London, Times Books.

Lown, J. (1983) 'Not so Much a Factory, More a Form of Patriarchy: Gender and Class during Industrialisation', in E.

Gamarnikov, D. Morgan, J. Purvis and D. Taylorson (eds) *Gender, Class and Work*, London, Heinemann.

Mant, A. (1977) *Rise and Fall of the British Manager*, London, Macmillan.

Marchant, H and B. Wearing (1988) (eds) *Gender Reclaimed: Women in Social Work*, Sydney, NSW, Hale & Iremonger.

Marshall, J. (1984) *Women Managers: Travellers in a Male World*, Chichester, John Wiley.

Maslow, A. (1943) 'A theory of human motivation', *Psychological Review*, no, 50.

May, R. (1972) *Power and Innocence*, London, Souvenir Press.

Meade-King, M. (1990) 'Making child care work', *Guardian*, 3 July.

Metcalf, H. (1990) *Retaining Women Employees: Measures to Counteract Labour Shortages*, IMS Report, no. 190, April, Falmer, Sussex.

Mihill, C. (1990) 'Girls feel terminal boredom thanks to computer bullies', *Guardian,* 25 August.

Miles, R. (1989) *A Woman's History of the World*, London, Paladin.

Municipal Year Book, 1951.

NALGO (National Association of Local Government Officers) (1989) *Social Work in Crisis*, NALGO.

National Council for Civil Liberties (now called Liberty) (1990) *No More Peanuts*, London, NCCL.

Nava, M. (1988) 'Cleveland and the press', *Feminist Review*, no. 28, January.

Neate, P. (1990) 'Men trapped in a spiral', *Community Care*, 27 September.

Nicholson, N. and M. West (1988) *Management Job Change: Men and Women in Transition*, Cambridge University Press.

Nice, V. (1988) 'Them and us: women as carers, clients and social workers', *Practice*, vol. 2, no. 1.

Novara, V. (1980) *Women's Work, Men's Work: The Ambivalence of Equality*, London, Boyars.

Oakley, A. (1974) *The Sociology of Housework*, Oxford, Robertson.

Oakley, A. (1979) *Becoming a Mother*, Oxford, Robertson.

Ogden, J. (1991) 'Society to advise sacked staff', *Social Work Today*, 8 August.

Painter, K. (1991) *Wife Rape, Marriage and the Law*, Research report commissioned by Granada TV.

Panos Institute (1991) *Triple Jeopardy: Women and AIDs*, London.

Pascall, G. (1986) *Social Policy: A Feminist Analysis*, London, Tavistock.

Pedler, M., J. Burgoyne and T. Boydell (1986) *A Manager's Guide to Self-Development*, New York, McGraw-Hill.

Pegg, M. (1990) *Lifeskills News*, Autumn.

Percival, L. (1989) 'Confronting gender issues', *Community Care*, 23.November.

Peter, L. (1971) *The Peter Principle: Why Things Always Go Wrong*, London, Pan.

Peters, T. (1987) *Thriving on Chaos*, London, Pan.

Peters, T. and R. Waterman (1983) *In Search of Excellence*, New York, Harper & Row.

Philips, A. and B. Taylor (1980) 'Sex and skill: notes towards a feminist economics', *Feminist Review*, no. 6.

Phillipson, J. (1990) 'Management is her story', *Social Work Today*, 5 April.

Phillipson, J. (1989) 'Race and Gender: A Woman's Chance to Choose', in T. Philpot (ed.), 'The Residential Opportunity? The Wagner Report and After', *Community Care*.

Phillipson, J. and M. Riley (1988) 'Experiences of Women Managers in Social Services', in P. Wedge (ed.), *Social Work – A Third Look at Research into Practice*, London, BASW–JUC.

Phillipson, J. and M. Riley (1990) 'Women for a change', unpublished M. Phil. thesis, Cranfield Institute of Technology.

Pizzey, E. (1974) *Scream Quietly or the Neighbours will Hear*, Harmondsworth, Penguin.

Platt, D. (1991) 'Squandered talent', *Social Work Today*, 8 August.

Popplestone, G. (1987) Unpublished paper.

Popplestone, R. (1979) 'The under-representation of women in senior management posts in SSDs', unpublished MA thesis, Brunel University, Uxbridge.

Popplestone, R. (1980) 'Top jobs for women: are the cards stacked against them?', *Social Work Today*, 23 September.

Popplestone, R. (forthcoming) *Women Managers: Finding an Easier Route Up the Ladder*, Social Services Research, University of Birmingham.

Pryde, K. (1991) 'Macho style represses passion', *Social Work Today*, 26 September.

Radford, M., J. Rose and G. Staniscia (1988) 'A woman's place?', *Social Work Today*, 17 November.

Rapoport, R. (1976) *Dual Career Families Revisited*, Oxford, Robertson.

Richards, M. (1990) Project for CCETSW on Competencies in Supervision, London, NISW.

Richards, M., C. Payne and A. Sheppard (1990) *Staff Supervision in Child Protection*, London, NISW.

Rickford, F. (1991) 'How could it happen?', *Social Work Today*, 5 December.

Rojak, C., G. Peacock and S. Collins (1988) *Social Work and Received Ideas*, London, Routledge & Kegan Paul.

Ross, J. (1990) 'Men manage while women work', *Community Care*, 8 November.

Rubenstein, M. (1988) *The Dignity of Women at Work: A Report on the Problem of Sexual Harassment in the Member States of the European Community*, COM v/412/1087, Brussels, Office for Official Publications of the European Commission.

Rubenstein, M. (1991) 'Devising a sexual harassment policy', *Personnel Management*, February.

Ruddock, M. (1990) 'Uncomfortable issues', *Community Care*, 4 October.

Ryan, M. and R. Fritchie (1982) Career Life Planning Workshops for Women Managers, Bristol Polytechnic/Manpower Services Commission.

Sainsbury, E. (1977) *The Personal Social Services*, London, Pitman.

Seebohm, F. (1968) *Report on Local Authority and Allied Personal Social Services*, London, HMSO.

Sinclair, I., R. Parker, D. Leat and J. Williams (1990) *The Kaleidoscope of Care*, London, HMSO.

Skelcher, M. (1987) 'Flexibility and Managing Our Boundaries', in J. Underwood (ed.), *Asserting the Female Perspective*, Working Paper No. 69, School for Advanced Urban Studies, University of Bristol.

Skinner, J. and C. Robinson (1988) 'Who Cares? Women at Work in Social Services', in A. Coyle and J. Skinner (eds), *Women and Work*, London, Macmillan.

Smithers, A. and P. Zlientek (1991) *Gender, Primary Schools and the National Curriculum*, London, NASUWT and. the Engineering Council.

Snowdon, R. (1980) *Aegis*, no. 29, Autumn.

SSI (Social Services Inspectorate) (1989) *Women as Managers*, London, HMSO.

SSI (Social Services Inspectorate) (1991) *Women in Social Services: A Neglected Resource*, London, HMSO.

Social Work Today (1990) 'Workers at risk', 19 July.

Social Work Today (1991) 'Notts bans abuse conference speech', 26 September.

Spence, J. and M. Sawbridge (1991) *The Dominance of the Male Agenda in Community Youth Work*, Dept of Adult and Continuing Education, University of Durham.

Spender, D. (1982) *Invisible Women*, London, The Women's Press.

Spender, D. (1985) *Man Made Language*, London, Routledge & Kegan Paul.

Springer, D. (1989) 'A lonely job at the top', *Community Care*, 31 August.

Statham, D. (1978) *Radicals in Social Work*, London, Routledge & Kegan Paul.

Statham, D. (1990) Unpublished paper presented to National Children's Homes and the Association of Directors of SSDs, November.

Steedman, J. (1983) *Examination Results in Mixed and Single Sex Schools: Findings from the National Child Development Study*, EOC.

Stewart, J. and M. Clarke (1990) *The New Management of Local Government*, London, Longman.

Stewart, J. and K. Walsh (1990) *The Search for Equality*, Luton, LGTB.

Stone, I. (1988) *Equal Opportunities in Local Authorities. Developing Effective Strategies for the Implementation of Policies for Women*, Manchester, EOC.

Surma, J. (1991) 'Community care is a women's issue A critical examination of the position and experiences of the informal carers of older women', dissertation, University of Warwick.

Thomas, B. (1987) 'Getting to the top', *Insight*, 11 September.

300 Group (1989) *Representation of Women at County Council Level in Local Government 1985–1989*, London.

Tolbert-Stroud, S. (1975) 'Working Black Women', in D. Jongeward and D. Scott (eds), *Affirmative Action for Women: A Practical Guide for Women and Management*, Reading, Mass., Addison-Wesley.

Trades Union Congress (1987) *Black and Ethnic Minority Women in Employment and Trade Unions*, TUC.

Treasury (1986) *Using Private Enterprise in Government*, London, HMSO.

Ungerson, C. (1983) 'Women and Caring: Skills, Tasks and Taboos', in E. Gamarnikow, D. Morgan, J. Purvis and D. Taylorson (eds), *The Public and the Private*, London, Heinemann.

Wainwright, H. (1978) 'Women and the Division of Labour', in P. Abrams (ed.), *Work, Urbanism and Inequality*, London, Weidenfeld & Nicolson.

Wagner, G. (1988) *Residential Care: A Positive Choice*, London, NISW–HMSO.

Walby, C. (1987) 'Why are so few women working in senior positions?', *Social Work Today*, 16 February.

Walton, R. (1975) *Women in Social Work*, London, Routledge & Kegan Paul.

Webb, M. (1982) 'The Labour Market', in I. Reid and E, Wormald (eds), *Sex Differences in Britain*, London, Grant McIntyre.

Wells, O. (1983) *Promotion and the Woman Probation Officer*, London, NAPO.

West Midlands County Council Women's Subcommittee (1985) Survey.

Weston, C. (1990) 'Lack of childcare confines women to marginal work', *Guardian*, 27 September.

White, A. (1989) *Poles Apart: The Experience of Gender*, London J. M. Dent.

Whitehorn, K. (1986) 'Does co-education just continue to stereotype your daughter? Is she better off at a single sex school?', *Observer*, 14 December.

Williams, L. (ed.) (1967) *Caring for People. Staffing Residential Homes*, London, George Allen & Unwin.

Williams, W. (1991) 'Ideal for the job', *Social Work Today*, 28 November.

Willis, M. (1990) 'Proportional representation', *Insight,* 24 October.

Wilson, E. (1977) *Women and the Welfare State*, London, Tavistock.

Women and Training (1991).

Wollard, J. and M. Lowe (1988) 'Women taking leadership in organisations', *Training Officer*, August.

Zimmerman, D. and C. West (1975) 'Sex Roles, Interruptions and Silences in Conversations', in B. Thorne and N. Henley (eds), *Language and Sex: Difference and Domination*, Boston, Mass., Newbury House.

Index